SERVING
IN
CLARITY

*A Guide for Lay Apostles
of Jesus Christ
the Returning King*

By Anne, a lay apostle

SERVING
IN
CLARITY

By Anne, a lay apostle

ISBN: 978-1-933684-89-5

Library of Congress Number: applied for

Publisher: Direction for Our Times
                    9000 West 81st Street
                    Justice, Illinois 60458

                    708-496-9300
                    www.directionforourtimes.org

Direction for Our Times is a 501(c)(3) tax-exempt organization.

Manufactured in the United States of America

Graphic design and stained glass art by:
                    Chris Deschaine
                    www.braintrustdesign.com

How to Pray the Rosary information and the image of *Mary Immaculate* are used with permission. Copyright © Congregation of Marians of the Immaculate Conception, Stockbridge, MA 01263. www.marian.org

Painting of *Jesus Christ the Returning King* by Janusz Antosz

I dedicate this book with gratitude to my husband, Jimmy.

Table of Contents

Part One

The New Time

August 7, 2006
Jesus

Be at peace in the sufferings that I send. My apostles in this time will carry crosses with Me, in all resignation. Through your docile acceptance of the cross, I will draw two things. One, I will make you a saint. Two, I will flow rich and constant graces through you into the world. You will be allowed to glimpse the fruit of your suffering at times. This will be a gift from Me, this knowledge of the connection between your offering and the fruits I send to the world. You will know that the peace and conversion of your family members and loved ones is connected to the crosses you carry in quietness. As grace flows into the world, through your souls and homes, those around you will begin to become holy, also. Their holiness will assist you and your holiness will continue to assist them and between us all we will have God's kingdom on earth. This is a summary of the new time and this time now is the beginning of the new time. The new time begins with a birth and that is the birth of great unity between God and man. Most births are joyous, it is true, but birth can also include some apprehension because birth is a beginning, something new. So it is with this time. Enhanced unity between God and His created ones is different in this time. It is new. There are always those saints who align their will to Mine and walk with Me but in this new time, most souls will live this way. We are not there yet, as you know, but we begin and we begin with you, My beloved apostles.

August 8, 2006
Jesus

Like heavenly ushers, My apostles escort Me into the world. I am the Returning King, after all, and all kings have their guards of honor. Will you join My guard, dear apostle? Will you walk closely alongside Me as I return to the world? Those who walk with the King are very close to His heart, of course. Because He spends so much time with these souls, there is familiarity between them. When one is familiar with another, in love, there is an easiness, a feeling of comfort in each other's company. That is what we have. We are comfortable together, are we not? We see each other's pain. We have also come to know what gives each other joy. I know what lifts your heart, My beloved one. I know what consoles you and gives you comfort. In the same way, you understand what consoles Me, what lifts Me and gives Me comfort. Shall I remind you? Love.

Love gives Me solace in a time when there is great hatred. I look to you and I see suffering, yes, pain, of course, but also love. I see that you suffer for Me and this sustains Me. I see your sacrifices and I see your wounds, and yet you continue to serve your King. You do not melt away into the world as others have. You do not allow your heart to be hardened as some do. You work constantly to allow Me access as the Divine Healer. I require constant access to your little heart, it is true, but you give that to Me

5

through your time in prayer and your willingness to be honest in assessing your actions and motives. Dearest apostle, walk with Me as one of My guards of honor. I love you immeasurably. I will care for everything and I will never fail to sustain you. Bring Me your fears constantly, in every moment. I will eradicate them. If you walk closely with Me, you will exert less effort and I will sow a heavenly garden in your soul as we proceed.

August 11, 2006
Jesus

The link between the Creator and the created must be intact. In this time, I intend to invite every soul to be connected personally with Me. You say, "This is so in every time. Why is this time different?" I will answer you in this way, My beloved apostles. The graces given now are unique to this time. There is a bond between us that insures our union. This is the result of grace from heaven and not from any extraordinary goodness on the part of humanity that is distinct from the goodness of souls in another time. Souls in other times possessed the graces necessary to serve in their time. Souls in this time will possess the graces necessary to serve in this time, if they desire these graces and if they desire to serve. I am responding to the time of darkness by initiating a time of great light. My apostles will have more direct contact with Me in their souls. I will manifest Myself differently to souls in this, the Advent of the Age of Obedience. This is another manifestation of My mercy, of course, and represents a heavenly concession to a humanity who has been badly confused by My enemy. My children were misdirected and allowed themselves to be moved from the heavenly course in the greatest numbers. Souls followed poor leaders and negative influences. Some souls remained true to My course. How I celebrate each and every one of you. How I rejoice for each of you. How the Trinity rushes to make a home in your little souls, so honest and true.

Falseness can not take root in you because you provide no home for the enemy's arrogance. Your Jesus will make you a great saint in return. Be assured that I am moving many souls in your direction now. You will be at home in heaven and you will be at home during your time on earth because I am in you and I will remain in you if you allow Me. Have courage. You are not alone in your faithfulness. Souls in great numbers join your ranks each day.

August 11, 2006
Jesus

There is quiet joy in service when this service is united to the Creator. There is steadiness of purpose and direction in the soul who toils alongside the King. This steady bearing is notable because it is a contrast to the inspirations that come from My enemy. When a soul is not linked to Me, that soul often lacks this steady bearing and the service of that soul is sporadic. When a soul lacks unity with Me, you will note bursts of heavenly service, followed by lapses of piety. This can be the way a soul behaves when that soul is new in service to the King. We must show compassion and love, but it is important that My beloved apostles who are experienced in service illustrate consistency. Always consider My will. In each moment look to your Returning King for instruction. I will have a purpose to each moment of your time on earth and it is necessary only for you to trust Me. There are many times when My purpose is obscured from you. Be at peace in this. You do not have to know what is in the King's mind once you know what is in the King's heart. I have only what is good in My heart. I have only what is best for you and for all those around you in My heart. Be at peace in each moment, relying on this truth. I hold the most perfect benevolence and compassion for each of My children on the earth. I have pledged to protect you in your service to Me. What should make you anxious? Nothing, My little one. Work steadily for heaven in service to Me and you will see My kingdom come through a steady effort.

August 14, 2006
Jesus

Listen to My words, beloved ones. You are special friends of the Savior. You are privileged to share My view of the world. Do not hold yourselves above others because of this. Rather, accept your role as the servant of others. You are My servant, are you not? You seek to further My goals? Then you must understand that you go out into the world as I went out into the world, as a humble truth-teller. I did not shout. I spoke gently and in the greatest love. You must do the same. Consider the knowledge you hold in your heart, where I have allowed the grace for understanding. Do others have the same graces? Do others benefit from the same understanding? Perhaps they do not. Perhaps they are not called to serve as you are called to serve so they are beginning and proceeding from a different point. Do not seek to be the master. I am the Master. Seek always to serve the Master and your struggle will be less.

August 15, 2006
Blessed Mother

This is the time of my Son. Dear apostle, how overjoyed I am at the loyalty He receives from this current band of followers. You are like apostles of the past in that you serve with consistency and joy. You are unique, though, given that you serve during a time when the enemy seeks to have a complete hold on this world. This attempt to overcome the world is bold. It insures that you will have to fight, as all apostles are called to fight. The difference for apostles in this time is the consistent level of resistance they face from the enemies of my Son. Consistent with the increased resistance is the increased grace, of course. Heaven and earth work together as in no other time. Yes, this is a time of great saints and great warriors but I speak of warriors not in the traditional sense of those who make and execute wars, but of those who fight and win the battle of the soul, which is the more difficult battle of overcoming self. I am so pleased with you. I am so grateful. A mother's gratitude overflows from her heart in both expected and unexpected gifts. Such graces and blessings I obtain for you, dear little apostle. I am the queen of all apostles and I am your queen. I am not a distant queen, detached and regal. I am the queen of your heart, present and approachable. I work with you continually, in each day, to help you carry out my Son's plan for you. Be quietly joyful on each day because your mother loves you and helps you in every moment.

August 17, 2006
Jesus

I am with you in each moment and you are listening for My Voice. This is good. This will work both for you and for heaven in terms of your growth and heaven's plan being furthered through you. The world shouts. I speak quietly. My apostles have learned to discern the difference between the voice of the enemy and the voice of the Savior. My apostles have learned to walk steadily despite the rushing of the worldly wind past their face. Such progress you make! Such advances! We are gaining ground in each moment, dear apostles. Be heartened by this and do not allow anyone to convince you otherwise. My renewal of this world is on target. I am at peace. I extend My peace to you, My loyal ones. In this time you will move steadily forward despite any traps or backlashes from My enemy. Forward. Confidence. Trust. It is My plan. I will execute it. You will assist Me in the manner I have revealed to you. You are prepared, have no fear. When you consider whether or not you are ready to execute your part in My plan, ask yourself this question. "Do I believe that Jesus Christ lives in Me?" If the answer is "yes," you are ready.

August 18, 2006
Jesus

Do not fear the battle, My beloved apostles. You suffer at times from feelings of emptiness. This emptiness is necessary. The more your soul is emptied of the things of this world, the more I can fill it with the things of the next world. This is a process. The word process implies change and change is necessary for the souls of My beloved apostles in order for them to be filled with Me exclusively. As this process advances, as the changes occur, you will find that I flow through you and out from you more freely, without any great effort on your part. My moving from your soul to the souls of others will become natural and effortless. It is this way for all truly dedicated apostles and it will be this way for you. Rejoice in this, even as it costs you some discomfort to abandon the ways of the world for the ways of the Savior. This is an answer to your prayers and an answer to the prayers of other apostles for you.

August 21, 2006
Jesus

My dear apostles of this time receive great courage from each other. At times you may feel as though you cannot continue in service because of the temptations and difficulties you must confront. At those times, look to others and see how they are proceeding. You will then sigh deeply, rest in My heart, and continue, knowing that others suffer alongside you. Others also struggle. Please believe that heaven is capable of sustaining you in even the harshest conditions. My beloved ones, please believe that heaven chooses to sustain you. It is heaven's choice that you persevere and with your willingness, you will persevere. If you fear that you are suffering too much, or that your path is too difficult, remember that you are surrounded by saints. They felt the same way at times. Remain in the present at each moment and you will find that peace is within you. I, Myself, will sustain you. That is My promise.

September 12, 2006
Jesus

Changes are coming. Humanity groans with the effort of altering its course. The change comes in the calmness of the souls of the just. Those who follow Me feel the stirring of hope and exhilaration. "Jesus is returning," they say in the silence of their hearts. Beloved ones, it is I who whispers to you. It is I who provides you with calm and peace. You know Me and you know My voice. Many of you dare not hope that your Savior is communicating with you in such intimacy. Be at peace. Trust My voice. You will hear Me in silence, of course, but you will confirm Me in the words that flow from you to others and in the love that moves through you to your brothers and sisters. You are changing. The world around you appears to be distressed, disturbed, and unsteady, but in the souls of My apostles there is a steady bearing that pushes My light across the earth. There is no stopping this renewal, My friend. Assist your Jesus to the fullest possible extent and you will realize your heavenly potential.

September 12, 2006
Jesus

There is joy, little apostles. I call you little apostles because a little apostle allows Me to become powerful in his soul. You will be exalted in heaven, My dear one. Be content to be small on earth. I see an army of apostles serving Me in this time. They are armed with truth and they are humble. What peace this brings the Savior. How easy it is for the Savior to flow through these ones who are comfortable with humility. Your eyes look ahead to the heavenly kingdom and in this way you serve steadily, connected to the Source of love. I rejoice in the kindness that others find in you. Dear apostles, it is My kindness that comes from you. You have graciously allowed Me to use you to return heavenly kindness to the world. You will not be sorry. Regret will not visit you upon your entry into the heavenly kingdom. You will be filled with joy and gladness as you are escorted into your eternity.

September 13, 2006
Jesus

Dear apostles, I love you. I love you perfectly and completely. My love for you never diminishes, despite any mistakes you may make. I am with you in each moment of your day. In each life there comes difficult moments and sorrowful situations. I am there, steadying you. I provide great graces when great graces are needed. Some souls reject Me and reject the graces I bring. Do I abandon those souls? Do I take My graces and turn My back? I tell you today, dear friends, I do not. I remain by that soul, giving graces freely despite their rejection. I do this because I long for each to turn to Me. I do this so that every soul, regardless of the darkness they are choosing, has something heavenly with which to compare the darkness. Do you understand? When you approach a soul who has rejected me, who lives in darkness, you bring a light which illuminates the grace all around that soul and that soul's life. You will never find a person living on earth who has no grace near them. The grace of the Father hovers nearby, always, ready to rush into the soul at the least openness. Therefore, walk in peace, of course, but also understand that all you need do is approach another. You carry My light within you. You cannot help but do this if you love Me and serve Me. Your very presence in a room will insure that others become aware, not only of the grace that surrounds you, but of the grace that surrounds them. No soul is abandoned while there is hope and hope re-

mains until a soul permanently rejects Me. Therefore, do not ever think that it is useless to bring Me to another, regardless of their condition. Please, contemplate this concept in silence and you will understand its power.

October 25, 2006
Blessed Mother

Little children, you are all safe in my Immaculate Heart. I am your mother. In a special way I protect you during this time. I shield you from influences that would lead you away from your path to my Son. You must cooperate with me so that I can protect you even more. Often a mother has information that her children do not need to know. A wise mother shares the information only when it is necessary to help her children identify danger. I am that way. I am sharing information now because I want you to know where the danger to your spirituality lies. It is good to listen to your mother because she seeks only what is good for you. I know that my Son's beloved apostles understand this and this is why I bring this information to you, asking you to spread it further for me.

Children, our enemy wishes to draw many souls into a Godless void. This is being done in a manner that is underhanded. If a person was asked directly, to reject God permanently, most would refuse. People do not want to permanently remove a chance to be with God, even if their faith is terribly weak and they never serve God at all. The enemy is not forthright, however, and souls are being deceived. You know this to a degree. I intend to advise you of a specific manner of conducting yourself so that I can protect you completely. In my Immaculate Heart you will find joy and peace. In my Immaculate Heart you will find comfort and gentle correction. I am your mother and I will help you.

October 26, 2006
Blessed Mother

Dearest children, I take great comfort in your fidelity to my Son. I would like for you to do the same. When you are tempted to become discouraged, look at the many apostles who remain faithful during this time. Look at the many who return to my Son through the efforts of these apostles. Look at the level of holiness that souls are achieving in short periods of time. Be consoled by these things as I am consoled by them. When you see falseness and you are tempted to be weighed down by it, understand that in the heavenly kingdom, all is truth. False writings, distorted theories and arguments quickly become nothings to be discarded by a world which moves swiftly from one error to the next. What stands, little apostles? What remains through time? God remains. God's truth remains. God's humble little serving apostles remain, rejoicing in their ultimate goal which is unity with Jesus, the beloved Savior. Walk past erroneous writings and teachings with a calm steady bearing. Your bearing leads to heaven. Worldly teachings are passing away and God's truth is spreading steadily, pausing for no man, no false teaching and no obstacle. You are on the side of unlimited power. Behave in all humility, according to this truth.

October 27, 2006
Blessed Mother

Dearest little apostles, be at peace in your weariness. Heaven understands that you sometimes feel tired. When you feel tired, you must understand that heaven is not tired. When you feel discouraged, you must understand that heaven is not discouraged. When you feel fear, you must understand that heaven is not afraid. If you need to rest, then rest for a time. Heaven will continue working, through you and all around you. I am speaking to you as a loving mother who understands your weariness. Whether you have worked long years for heaven or are just beginning the work of the divine, you will experience fatigue. Be at peace in this. It does not mean you are unsuited to the work or that the work is unsuited to you. It means simply that you are tired.

October 31, 2006
Blessed Mother

Dearest apostles, I am filled with hope as I see you serving. How heaven rejoices in this new band of faithful servants. Many of you have been called from the world and from worldly pursuits because we are asking that you serve in the world. Your experience of the world will help you to understand how best to communicate with others who live outside of heaven's goals. Please do not worry about the sins of your past. God forgives. If you confess these sins, Jesus forgives and sends healing graces. You will then be free of them. Understand that Jesus wants you to be free of your sins and it is His will that you accept the forgiveness that He makes available in this holy sacrament. Rejoice in this forgiveness and mercy and do not fret over your past. If you continue to fret over your past mistakes, the enemy can create a hold on you. Jesus died for your sins and He did this so that you could be free of them. Rejoice, dear little apostles. Jesus loves you and counts you as His friend. He will forget your mistakes. So must you.

November 2, 2006
Blessed Mother

God's little apostles are part of a heavenly team that does not pause. The team pushes God's message further and further into the world. The team supports each other and encourages each other. The team members point always to Jesus when their fellow apostles become discouraged or distracted. God's truth gives such joy and it is in reminding each other of God's truth that you will sustain each other. When a friend and fellow apostle is discouraged, you must remind God's servant that he works for the cause of the Returning King. There is only one truth and one King, after all. If you are called to this mission, you are called to serve completely. Give your heart to my Son and allow Him to use you to heaven's fullest advantage. Do not be distracted by those who doubt your commitment. Serve in steadiness, understanding that you have been given many experiences and graces to allow you to serve as God needs you to serve in this time. Do not be like the ones who accepted God's healing but failed to thank Him. Everything you have has been given to you by God. Use everything you have to help heaven to prepare the world for the return of my Son.

November 3, 2006
Blessed Mother

Can you think of yourselves as my little children? Try to do this. If you begin to think of yourselves as my little children, you will begin to understand that you have a heavenly mother who protects you. Also, I send all guidance to you. Perhaps you are fearful and apprehensive about the work the Lord is asking you to do. Dearest apostles, is it not natural to take any apprehensions to your mother? With me you will find reassurance and understanding. With me you will find new courage and determination. Truly, when I ask you to think of yourself as my little son or daughter, I speak the truth. You are my son. You are my daughter. I am your mother. I am also the mother of Jesus so we are all in the same family. I work only for the goals of my Son. You will never find that my guidance takes you away from the will of God. This would be impossible. As Jesus' mother, I look out for His objectives in every situation. As your mother, I will look out for your well-being in every situation, but also, I will look out for the well-being of God's plan. Allow me to help you as a mother helps and you will find a new confidence.

November 11, 2006
Blessed Mother

Little apostles, gather near me in your hearts. I work tirelessly to keep you, my faithful little children, together so that you can console and help each other. In this way, you are sustained and encouraged. You understand that heaven is with you. Heaven understands that it is good for you to have earthly fellowship also. Take care of these relationships with your fellow apostles. Treat each other gently as Jesus treated everyone He encountered on earth. Those around you will make mistakes and fall victim to their weaknesses. When this occurs, you must rejoice in the opportunity to show God's mercy to them. You must rejoice in the opportunities to be forgiving. You must bring any anger or hurt to me and I will help you with it so that you can grow from it, benefiting heaven from your offerings to Jesus in the face of your pain. If you do this, offer your hurts to heaven, we can send great blessings on you, on the fellow apostle who has hurt you, and, indeed, on the whole mission throughout the world. This mission is fuelled by littleness, by humility. Seek out humility and you will find it. You will then be gentle as Jesus is gentle. Keep humility close to you as your most trusted friend because in humility you will find a clearsightedness that allows you to keep God's goals in the first place of all of your service. Dearest apostles, little children, what joy there is for me to teach you about heaven and heavenly behavior. These words and graces are a great gift to your world and your reading of these words is a great gift to me, your heavenly mother.

Part Two

The Lay Apostle Call

Duty

September 18, 2006

This morning I had quite a few tasks to accomplish. There were so many that I did not know where to begin. My head was stuffed with them all. I closed my eyes for the briefest moment and said, "Jesus, I know You are with me. What do *You* want me to do first?" Immediately my thoughts went to a file that needed editing and completion. I knew in my heart that Jesus wanted me to finish that job first and then move on to other things.

To clarify, this was after I had risen, offered God my day, fed my children and dressed them and gotten them off to school, gone to Mass, cleaned my house, and then come in to work. My point is that my duties came first.

There is no need for discernment if there are children to be fed or cared for or a house to be cleaned or a professional job to be at. The Lord wishes to help us discern at each moment where we feel uncertainty. We will then serve the Lord as He wishes, saying "no" to our will and "yes" to His.

September 20, 2006

Yesterday was a dark day in terms of the cross. This morning, I rose with a continued feeling of discouragement and blackness. In my heart and mind I experienced no light. I looked at those around me and could see only their flaws and weakness, along with my own. I wondered how on earth the Lord would pull us together and get any good from us. I looked also at those who were called to serve but who had fallen away.

I then considered the world where goodness is mocked and condemned. In its place the world elevates and applauds selfishness and base behavior. Those who truly represent Christ are targeted by even some who purport to serve Him because in their hearts they serve themselves. Such duplicity! Falseness! Contempt for innocence! How on earth are we to proceed in such an environment?

I went to Mass seeking the One I cannot find. There was no Mass. A man also seeking Christ this morning winked at me and said, "We should have read the bulletin." His friendliness allowed the smallest bit of light into my heart.

Jesus, who hides from me, began to speak. He said, *"Anne, come home to Me and write. The enemy plans destruction. I, in My mercy, plan salvation for My children. This consoles Me."*

Back at home, I closed my eyes at the request of the Savior, listening to His voice. I experience no joy from this. It is like getting a telegram in the sense that I am denied any consolation from it. God wills this for many reasons at this time, the most important of which is that I must experience these moments exactly as other lay apostles experience them. I rested in my misery. Jesus told me to pray.

I said, "Lord, please give me renewed courage. Send me greater strength. Give me clarity in my role in the kingdom on this day so that I may not disappoint you."

I lifted my head and began to write and as I did, I felt a return of courage and strength. I actually felt I could continue where prior to the prayer, I really felt I would lay my head down and quit.

Jesus said this: *My apostles will be sustained. Have no fear that I will allow an apostle to perish in battle. I will sustain My apostles with a constant stream of courage and strength in this new time, insuring that each apostle desiring to serve will have exactly the graces needed to do so. Anne, these words should fill each apostle with joy. When the Savior Himself makes a promise to those who serve Him, He will go to any lengths to fulfill His pledge. Apostles will experience My assistance in countless ways. This morning another apostle transmitted courage to you by his cheerfulness in the face of disappointment. Have no fear that you will be overcome. I will sustain you.*

Truth

September 21, 2006

There was a story about a vain emperor. In order to gain favor with him, some unscrupulous ones persuaded the leader to proceed naked. Being a foolish man, the emperor allowed himself to be influenced by the flattery of those around him. He proceeded through his kingdom naked. Because of his power, nobody had the courage or mercy to speak the truth, which was that the emperor was wearing no clothes. Instead, they allowed him to humiliate himself. A small child with clear vision finally spoke up and said, "The emperor is wearing no clothes."

There is a similar phenomenon in this time. Truth is often not spoken. This habit of keeping back the truth has allowed God's enemy terrific latitude in spreading sin and immorality. In the essay entitled *Common Sense*, written by Thomas Paine, we read that "a long habit of not thinking a thing *wrong*, gives it a superficial appearance of being *right*, and raises at first a formidable outcry in defense of custom."

So pervasive is this phenomenon that there is a name for it. It is called political correctness. I will take license and translate this term. Let us consider political correctness as a decision not to speak a truth if that truth will offend the sensibilities of those whose favor we seek.

In other words, it would not be politically correct to share our honest feelings if our honest feelings would put us in bad favor with others. To be clear, it is not a decision to hold back the truth in order to avoid hurting the feelings of another, but a decision to hold back the truth to prevent reprisals of some kind.

Hmm. How does this compare to the kingdom of God?

The Kingdom of God, in my experience, is all about truth. This truth is not negotiable and it does not change. Bad behavior is bad behavior and a bad behavior today does not become a good behavior tomorrow when we look at the spirit of the said behavior. How could it? Sin, a decision to separate oneself from God's will, is known as sin in God's kingdom and none will spend time in heaven or purgatory trying to decide if a sin was a sin.

If we search high and low in the next world, we will not find political correctness.

What will we find?

We will find truth, which is sometimes the opposite of political correctness. From the Christian point of view, which is the point of view Christians must operate from, it is merciful to speak the truth in love. In this time, there will be people who can justly stand up and say, "Nobody told me I was committing sin." Those of us around these people who are proceeding in ignorance, particularly family members, may be accountable if we fail to offer loving correction.

How does one share the truth?

As lay apostles, we look always to the example of Jesus Christ in Scripture. First of all we ask ourselves if Jesus was politically correct. Did our Jesus hold back the truth so that people would like Him and not kill Him? No. Jesus Christ spoke the truth in the greatest gentleness and love. He spoke the truth as a teacher speaks the truth, with a goal of illuminating the soul of the person with whom he speaks, thus advancing that person so that the person can go on to accept even greater truths.

Did Jesus say, "I know the truth and you do not, therefore I am better than you?"

Did Jesus say, "I live the truth and you do not, therefore I am going to heaven and you are not?"

Did Jesus say, "If you don't immediately conform to My exact view of the truth you will go to hell?"

Clearly not. It is not Jesus who speaks like this.

Remember that Jesus had the complete truth. He was the Truth then and He is the Truth now, and yet, from this position of power Jesus was and is gentle and kind. We, His followers, are called to proceed similarly. We must speak the truth in kindness and gentleness, remembering always that we do not hold ourselves above anyone.

I have observed some misguided apostles proceeding in great superiority to those around them. They are arrogant and give reprimands to others freely, as though they themselves had no spiritual work to do. This is wrong and it saddens Christ. The recipient of this kind of treatment feels rejection and condemnation, two things that do not come from Christ, but from His enemy.

I hear the voices of these same people shouting, "But souls **are** condemned. There **are** souls in hell."

This is true, but the souls in hell are there because they choose hell, not because God rejects them or condemns them. God is good and gives all people an opportunity to repent. We must be humble, as Jesus was humble, and bring a spirit of loving truth to others. If we do this, souls will recognize God's mercy in us and they will return to Him, not from fear, but from love and because they have been welcomed.

In the greatest humility and love, dear apostles, speak the truth if the Holy Spirit asks you to do so.

September 26, 2006

It can be difficult to speak the truth. It can be frightening. God will give us the courage we need, though, if we ask Him. God will not abandon us to the falseness of the world. When the world around us is proceeding in greater truth than falseness, we will know that God's kingdom comes.

Look for opportunities to share God's truth in the world. I believe that we will find such opportunities in each day.

God's truth must be seen as an honest appraisal of a given thing.

Each apostle must spend a certain amount of time daily appraising the truth of his own actions and motives. We should not drive ourselves distracted with our flaws, but neither should we be timid about self-examination. Only if we are honest with ourselves will we become able to help others.

We must look now at a truth that we often discount. What is the truth about the commitment of those around us? Look hard at those with whom you walk through life. Isn't it true that many serve with great steadiness? Isn't it true that many love Jesus and seek to live in accordance with that love, despite periodic failure?

If the truth of these statements is distasteful to us, or we are inclined to reject it, we must examine the possibility that we are looking only for flaws in our companions. We must spend time looking at the truth which is that many people in the world respect God's dominion over the world. Many people serve their families or live their religious vocations with great commitment and love. Living one's vocation with commitment and love is what we seek to achieve. If a person is doing so, we can be assured that his service is pleasing to God.

It is a possible snare for apostles to use the flaws of others to elevate themselves in their own eyes and, God help them, in the eyes of the world.

"He is bad, therefore I am good."
"He is not serving well, therefore I am superior."
"I am very holy because he is not very holy."

The frailties and weaknesses of another may keep that person out of heaven but that is between that person and God. What we can say for certain is that the frailties and weaknesses of others will not get us into heaven. When we face God and account for our life, we will not be able to produce other people's sinfulness as evidence of our holiness. We will stand alone, accounting for the way in which we behaved.

As apostles, we must flee from any type of smug thinking. I have said this before in other places but I will continue to say it because it is dangerous and destructive in terms of both our personal movement to holiness and the coming of God's kingdom.

When we find ourselves considering the unworthiness, sinfulness, or mistakes of another, we must get silent immediately, lest we do damage to the other person or to his reputation. Then we must beg Jesus to enlighten our own soul in order that we see where we need to improve. If we do this, we will become as holy as we should.

Consider a woman examining her neighbor's garden with the greatest disdain. She remarks to others that her neighbor has weeds around her rose bushes, overgrown grass, and unswept and untidy sidewalks. She tsk tsk tsks that women today do not seem to care about their duty. She points to one small area of her own garden that is tidy and uses this to show others how dutiful she herself is. The back of her house, however, is a disastrous mess with overgrown bushes, tall grass, and refuse strewn all over. Additionally, the inside of her house is disorderly and cold.

Does she see to her own mess? No. She stands facing her neighbor's garden. She points continually to the one small area of her yard that looks clean so that others will both admire her and denounce the neighbor.

To be clear, I am speaking in a metaphor. The garden I refer to is actually the soul of the woman in question. She is so busy criticizing her neighbor that she pays no heed to the work she herself needs to do.

Before any of us enter heaven, we will have to be honest about our flaws. We can do the work here or in the hereafter but God is clear that He wants us to do this honesty work here.

September 27, 2006

I sat down to work. It occurred to me that I wanted everything I wrote to be blessed by heaven. I felt the need and desire to allow heaven to use me in purity. This was a special job that I was beginning, even though it was part of the work that I do each day. I needed the Lord to come into it powerfully, though, so I paused and did a brief spiritual communion.

I prayed simply, "Through the intercession of Mary, Queen of Apostles, please grant me the grace of a spiritual communion."

I then began to speak to Jesus, telling Him about what I was working on and asking Him to take responsibility for it and protect the project through an outpouring of grace. I silently considered what I needed to do and how heaven would like to see it go. This recollected me and I began.

Jesus as the Good Shepherd

October 30, 2006

In the church where I often pray, there is a large stained glass window above the altar on the wall. In it is Jesus as the Good Shepherd. My eyes often rest on this beautiful image.

On His shoulder, Jesus carries a lamb. The lamb is right up against the Lord's head, with his little face resting against the face of Jesus. The lamb fits perfectly into the shoulder and neck of the Shepherd. The lamb looks safe and comfortable and the large steady hand of the Shepherd can be seen holding the lamb securely.

I often reflect on this.

Surely the lamb was dirty and soiled, given that he was plucked from a field where he had gotten lost. Also, when a lamb is lifted up from one place and pulled into human arms to be taken to another place, the lamb sometimes reacts badly and struggles or fights. This could result in injury to the shepherd, even unintentional injury because the animal, in its ignorance and fear, might not understand that the shepherd seeks to rescue and protect. Given the risk of injury, it would be understandable if the shepherd held the animal away from himself.

Does Jesus, the Good Shepherd, hold us away from Himself?

No. The image has accurately captured the feelings Jesus has for each one of us. Jesus pulls us in, close against Himself, even though in doing so the Lord risks injury.

And it is true that we often wound Jesus. We wound Him intentionally, through sin, and unintentionally, through neglect and mistrust.

Think for a moment. How many people do we allow to rest

their faces against ours? I imagine there are not many adults with whom we are so comfortable that we allow such intimacy. Clearly, we are more comfortable with a baby pressing his face against ours or a small child doing so. This is because of their innocence. We know they have no bad agenda for us. Any harm the infant does is accidental.

This is the way Jesus proceeds with each one of us. He pulls us in closely against His very face. He views us as His children, His little infants. He accepts the harm we may do to Him because it is so important that we are near Him and that we are safe.

It is true that the shepherd cannot stop a lamb that struggles violently and leaps from His arms. In this case, the Good Shepherd simply goes after the lamb, attempting again and again to bring the lamb to safety.

This image speaks to me each day. It gives me great courage and comfort. We want to be those who kiss and caress the face of Christ in return for His willingness to love us so tenderly, even with our sins and self-will.

The Invisible Reality

October 30, 2006

God is real.

I know this. There is an Invisible Reality that includes God, the kingdom of God, the family of God, the Body of Christ, the Communion of Saints, and our brothers and sisters being purified in purgatory. We are all connected and interconnected by the Spirit that is God's power and movement and presence in the world.

Souls are drawn to God by this Invisible Reality. What is it? What does this mean?

I believe that the Invisible Reality is truth. Truth is and always will be. Like God, truth cannot be altered or changed. It remains. Truth encompasses all of the universe, all of the souls ever created. Truth includes the reality of all sin, yes, but also the reality of every act of mercy, of merit and goodness. These positive acts make reparation for sins. Christians are asked to give their whole lives to this Invisible Reality.

Why would we? Why do we? What is it that compels us to follow the carpenter's Son?

I believe that we have an interior knowledge and memory of truth. The world seeks to upend it or destroy it, dull it, refute it, confuse it, but I believe that deep inside, people know that God exists and that there is a perfect truth.

Sometimes we are more able to judge something by its opposite and this is true with truth. The opposite of truth, falseness, is revolting to a servant of God.

Falseness leaves one confused. Truth leaves one certain.

Falseness leaves one anxious. Truth leaves one calm.

Falseness makes people feel unloved. Truth makes people understand that they are cherished and of infinite value.

The opposite of holiness is arrogance and superiority.

If the Invisible Reality is truth, and encompasses all unseen spiritual reality, we understand that nothing can add to it or detract from it. On earth, we are allowed more or less knowledge of it, depending on God's will for us and our cooperation with God's will for us. Some work happily for the Invisible Reality with a very little amount of revelation. How pleasing these people are to our God.

In heaven, we will have a perfect knowledge and what was concealed will be revealed. The Invisible Reality will be visible in terms of knowledge and vision. No longer will we be asked to proceed in the Invisible Reality. Instead we will be allowed to remain in the Visible Reality that is the heavenly kingdom.

How do we know that the Invisible Reality exists when we can't see God?

Why do we construct a windmill when we cannot see the wind? Do we ridicule those who go sailing? Isn't it true that men have sailed the seas for years relying only on the power of the wind? Which one of those men could see the wind?

We have all heard this comparison before but I repeat it as it works.

How many of us will get up in the morning and hang wet clothes on a rope outside of our back doors? Will anyone doubt that we are sensible in doing so? Will they say our hope is fanciful and childish and foolish? No. They will also hang clothes on the line if they are not using their clothes dryers.

Those who have gone before us knew something that we also know. Wind exists. It is real.

My friends, in the same way, God is real. We cannot see

Him. It is true. He limits our vision during our time on earth. Let everyone, in silence, ask themselves to consider a time when they KNEW God was with them.

Perhaps it was a moment, an impression, a feeling of being loved in the soul. Perhaps it was a feeling that someone who had gone before us was with us, helping or consoling. I am not talking about a frightened feeling but a calm certainty that we were not alone, not abandoned, and that we were connected to something invisible and very, very, big.

We must rely on our experience of the effect of God, the effect of prayer and grace.

If we hang wet clothes on the line and there is wind, the clothes will dry. There is a difference, a change. Wet clothes become dry.

In the same way, spending time with God in prayer brings change. We become calmer, more recollected. The world and those in it begin to look differently. Our vision shifts and alters from the earthly view to the heavenly view.

Instead of thinking like worldly souls, who base their life on what can be seen, we begin to think more like saints, who base their life on what they cannot see, the Invisible Realty.

The more we pray, the more confidently we function in and cooperate with the Invisible Reality.

Let it be said that God is never confused. God is never unsure or doubtful, fearful or full of hate. Through prayer we receive God's clarity of thought. If we spend time in prayer with God, we will understand what others understand and that is that God loves us and God is with us in each moment.

Truly, God is good. Serving God brings joy and peace, comfort and confidence. Serving God brings hope and trust, and a calm purpose.

Of course, there are those who mock people who pray. People laugh at them.

Dear friends, Christians have always been mocked. Identifying oneself as a Christian insures that we are targets, just as Christ was and is a target. Those who do not follow God, who are suffering from the pain of isolation from God, tend to strike out at followers. When we call ourselves Christians, we will be held to a higher level. There is an expectation that we will be kinder and more Christ-like. When we fail, others scoff and ridicule. But Jesus Himself fell. Jesus does not ridicule us. He offers us a hand and pulls us back to our feet.

I see it this way. If an apostle were going sailing, he would prepare his boat. Perhaps someone approaches him as he prepares his boat and says, "You cannot sail that boat. There is no such thing as wind."

The apostle would say, "I believe in wind."

"That's childish, foolish. Where is this wind? Produce it. I cannot see it and neither can you."

The reply? "I have seen the effect of the wind. I have felt the wind. The wind has helped me and others sail in the past and I believe that if I am patient, the wind will eventually fill my sails and take me further along the course I have set for my boat."

The scoffer remarks, "You fool. You will be sitting in that harbor all day. We are having a party and you are missing it."

This is rather obvious because we all know that the wind will blow and the boat will sail.

But maybe it will not be exactly according to the goals of the apostle. Maybe the apostle has to rely on the timing of the wind as opposed to the wind relying on the timing of the apostle. Sometimes apostles end up in places where they did not think they were going or where they did not want to go. And sometimes apostles get stuck in a place and they simply have to wait.

But wind is real. And so is God.

How do we prepare for sailing or advancing in faith?

First, we must get into our boats. In terms of faith, this is what I mean.

We are Catholics. We believe that Jesus Christ came. We believe He died, and then rose from the dead. He started one Church and it is the Catholic Church. We have direct succession from St. Peter all the way down to our beloved Pope Benedict XVI. Catholics, be Catholic. May God's peace extend to all other religions, but let us, as Catholics, learn about our own faith. Let us rejoice in the fullness of the Catholic truth. Let us stop pointing at what our brothers and sisters in the Church did wrong and scrutinize our own souls and our own performance for heaven and for the Church.

In the name of Jesus, we must reject the spirit of disobedience that blows through the world and through our Church.

We, as lay apostles, are called to be followers in God's Church. A lay apostle of Jesus Christ the Returning King should be known for his fidelity to the Magisterium of the Church. If we follow in the spirit of obedience, others will follow, and gradually the Body of Christ will move away from the current destructive spirit of disobedience.

We, lay apostles serving in our humanity, have made mistakes and will continue to make mistakes. For this reason, we adhere to God's guideline that we go to Confession once a month. This is how we keep our course set for heaven.

If we are trying to learn about and follow our Catholic faith, we are in our boat, preparing to sail.

Next, we must put our sails up.

To raise our sails, we pray. Each time we pray we are harnessing the power of God. Through prayer, the wind blows and our boat begins to move. The more we pray, the faster we move. Picture a sailor's face in the wind, hand on the tiller, with his boat moving steadily and swiftly toward his destination. What joy is in this image! What peace! This is an invigorating thought and must fill us with a determination to commit to prayer, thus harnessing God's power for our own movement to holiness and for the grace of conversion for others.

November 1, 2006

Each day we should examine our Invisible Reality. What is real to us that we cannot see? What decisions have we made for our life based on our Invisible Reality? How must we live those decisions on each day?

As I have said, I believe there is one God and one truth. On earth, people disagree over what they believe is truth, contrasting it to what others believe is truth. I believe that people can have a different vantage point of the truth, along with a different measure or amount of the truth, but I do not believe that truth can change. Truth is objective.

Someone once asked me why God reveals Himself more to some than others. I wondered about this for a moment. The answer came quite quickly.

Each soul is different, with different capabilities and a different intended plan for his service to the kingdom. This plan is adapted daily, as in his free will an individual serves or does not serve.

If a person is not disposed to gain from and make use of exceptional graces, what benefit is there for either the individual or the kingdom in giving that person such graces?

The Lord does not send mystical experiences without reason. Those who experience the mystical are heavily obligated. If one person is given more divine knowledge than another, we can bet that more will be expected of him in terms of service and sacrifice. There will be divine accountability.

Who would ask to be more accountable than another? Not I, dear friends, and neither should you.

We must always be looking to expand our Invisible Reality, but respectfully so. We should not ask for extraordinary mystical experiences. This would be foolish and possibly done with flawed motive. Instead we should ask for ordinary graces and blessings which will increase our knowledge of the character of our good God. Think in terms of what will help us to love Jesus more and move us further up the mountain of holiness. Think always in terms of an increase in personal holiness. We must ask for the grace to be humble so that God can be majestic.

Dear apostles, with great conviction, I believe Jesus is asking us to push past our limits of service.

There is a line we have drawn in our heads and the line represents our "this far and no further" mark. In this time, in this apostolate, we are called to gently step beyond that line as Christ draws us. This is not a glory-filled, noisy charge made amongst cheering multitudes. On the contrary, this is a weary "one step further for Christ" increase. This is a sometimes tear-filled, sometimes nearly broken, and usually fear-filled "YES" to the Lord that draws us past our intended limit of service.

Such fear! Such trepidation!

But Jesus will not see us perish and it can be stated that there are times when the act of clinging to this truth is the only means of buoyancy we possess.

How vulnerable we are in our lack of trust, but how grateful is Jesus for our willingness to serve.

November 2, 2006

A fellow apostle pointed out that much of our reality is invisible. As an example, he said, "Have you ever seen Australia?
"No," I replied. "I have never seen Australia."
"Do you believe it exists?"
"Yes," I said. "I believe Australia exists."
"Are you reasonably certain Australia exists?"
"Yes."
"You believe Australia exists, in part, because you are relying on the testimony of those who have been there. Others have told you Australia exists. You have read about Australia, seen pictures of it perhaps, and your belief in its existence is reasonable given the evidence."

This spoke powerfully to me. I realized that if asked, I could give a certain amount of testimony about Australia despite never having been there. I believe there are kangaroos there, different seasons, crocodiles, vast expanses of unsettled land, and a good number of people with Irish ancestry. Additionally, I am aware of the Aborigine people native to that land. I understand, based on what I have seen of the Australians I have met personally, that there is a great sturdiness and resilience in the Australian people.

Clearly I am not an expert on Australia. As I said, I have never been there. That fact will be evident to any Australian reading this. My limited knowledge of Australia comes in part from the testimony and information given to me by other people.

So it is with heaven. So it is with Jesus and with God's truth.

A good part of the truth, the Invisible Reality that we rely on and believe in, has come to us from others in the Body of Christ, the community of believers. We accept the testimony of others because in our souls, we recognize the truth. This is discernment. In the same way, with the help of the Holy Spirit, we are led to recognize what is false.

Holiness in Relationships

Sunday November 12, 2006

It is clear to me that people around us can be the cause of great upset. When a spirit is striving for God's calm and a steady bearing, the enemy will sometimes allow someone close to him to disturb him and cause his spirit to become upset. An upset spirit is discouraging but we can use these experiences to advance our humility.

Perhaps someone around us is behaving in a hypocritical manner. Perhaps we are the only ones who know this to be true. Perhaps this person is unkind to us and cruel, but only when others cannot see and often under a pretense of helping us or instructing us. They hold themselves far above us in their hearts. They will knock us down in order to build themselves up. They slap out at us to confirm their own worth. They do not do this directly or in a spirit of truth, but indirectly, under subterfuge, pouncing on our faults and then communicating these faults, greatly inflated, to others in such a way as to distort the truth. These people delight in any mistakes we make, hurriedly reporting them to others so as to increase the esteem others have for them by decreasing the esteem others have for us.

This can make us feel confused, uncertain, angry, depressed, and sad. It can begin to consume us and disturb our peace to a degree that makes it nearly impossible to continue on in life alongside them. The spirit of untruth about them upsets us and we begin to look constantly for evidence of the bad spirit to confirm to us that we are correct and justified.

This reality seeking is necessary for a time to confirm that we are indeed dealing with a person who is false and behaving like a Pharisee but it must be limited. I am saying that at some point we must say, STOP, to ourselves. We must resist the temptation to fall into the same trap by looking more at their misbehavior than at our own mountain paths.

One thing for certain is that the Lord will deal with the sins of others. None of us will escape the spirit of truth from illuminating our hearts. We must look at the person honestly, understanding that we are dealing with a spirit of untruth. We must pray for them. We should refuse to enter into the spirit of untruth. We should be kind, thanking Jesus for helping us to determine the difficulty. We should also pray that God releases us from obsessing about the person and the situation. Jesus will free us when it is good for us to be free.

We must be vigilant that we do not walk down this path ourselves. If we detect feelings in ourselves of envy and jealousy toward another, we must pray that Jesus deliver us and also protect the other person. There is no need to be jealous as the Lord loves us each completely. What will please our Jesus is a determination to do our own work and not cause scandal to another by illuminating their faults when there is no justifiable need.

It is true that people like this can do some damage but it is also true that Jesus Christ protects His apostles. Be assured that the Lord will limit the damage done to our movement to holiness and our reputations. If we walk in unity with the Lord in these situations, He can make us very holy, very fast.

Consider that each interaction with someone like this is like attending an Olympic-level holiness camp. Such opportunity! Truly, the saints would thank Jesus for allowing it.

We may not be quite there yet. We may be tempted to throw our hands up in disgust at our inability to remain holy in the face of such a challenge.

Be at peace, fellow apostles. Jesus allows this for our humility and it is entirely possible that our example will be beneficial to this person. At the very least, if we accept these situations, trusting Jesus, our peace will be protected.

November 13, 2006

About trusting Jesus in these situations, I would like to say this. It is in this trust that we are liberated from unruliness in our spirits and bitterness in our hearts. Let us consider our fears and how the enemy inflates them.

As stated, these persons can do damage to our reputations and the esteem others feel for us. So what? Wasn't Christ slandered in the same way? We must give Jesus our reputations and allow Him to see to the regard others have for us. A holy and humble apostle said recently that we must remember that by following Mary, the Blessed Mother, we are following a woman who could have been perceived by others as an unwed mother from Nazareth. If the false condemnation of others will damage God's plan, He will not allow it. We must trust the Lord to protect His interests and be at peace in any suffering He allows for us in these matters.

It is true that their treatment feels like exploitation. It seems that we are objects used by them to feed their egos. We can feel we are used by them to be the mirrors in which they admire themselves. We feel the indifference in their hearts, even when their words express great love and affection. Their professed love feels like a cruel lie. Recipients of this feel tremendous revulsion.

As a child I experienced adults who pretended to love but did not love in reality. Their affection stopped cold when their audience disappeared. I remember the acute disgust I felt at the duplicity of these adults. Children are excellent at distinguishing between authentic love and false or self-serving love. Because they themselves operate in a spirit of truth, they can readily identify who loves them and who is disinterested in them.

Be alert to this serious potential snare. We must never hold ourselves above those around us even when we are hurt by them. That would put us perilously near to climbing into the same boat.

It is apparent that the Lord wills a spirit of self-knowledge for each of us. As lay apostles, we must be willing to do the hard work in our souls. Our motives must be pure for our consciences to be clear. As my friend said, the enemy comes from within and without. God's enemy can advance in us if we entertain impure motives. May God give us the desire to work hard with Him at purifying our motives.

When one's motives are selfless, each day is viewed as an equally attractive opportunity for service to God's kingdom. There is little rising and let down. Service done in the company of only heaven will seem as alluring as service seen by multitudes here on earth and service done in the presence of the multitudes on earth will seem as alluring as service done in the company of only heaven.

Oh my friends, let us pray daily that the Lord nourish in us a great detachment from the opinions of others. If we arrive at this detachment, it will be difficult for the enemy to knock us off our paths. We will serve in a spirit of clarity and peace. We will trust our Jesus, who conquered the world, to protect us from the false motives of those around us.

Humility

On most mornings, I present myself to God in Mass and pray. There are many times, perhaps most times, when I do so with the awareness that I, myself, have nothing to offer the kingdom. I tell our Father that I am empty, without merit or hope of merit. I then ask our good God to fill me with Himself so that I can serve within the stream of His light and will.

There was a time when this prayer was made in desperation. I noted my emptiness in near panic as I understood that God had plans for me on the given day. Not anymore. I present myself to Him each morning in a spirit of peace about my emptiness. If I am empty, if I have nothing to offer, how much more efficiently can the Lord fill me with His goals and inspirations.

On this morning, I presented myself in some distress. I was aware that not only was I empty, devoid of all good inspirations, but I had a surplus of negative inspirations and feelings, consistent more with God's enemy than with God. I presented myself as a construction job for Jesus, or more accurately, an excavation task. I urgently needed Jesus to clear out the debris of a period of upset that had thrown me into the state of unruliness formerly mentioned.

This is good to mention and I do so in obedience to the wishes of the Creator. It is good because we must all be fearless in the face of our weakness and propensity for sin. My prayer this morning was tinged with fear, I will admit, given that I, like all of us, am called to be an apostle. The enemy uses this fear to taunt us by planting thoughts.

My dear friends, I was scheduled to speak one day. Before I rose, this conversation was going through my head:

"You are no apostle. A holy apostle of God does not harbor such feelings. You are not only unworthy, you are dangerous to God's plan. You are doing damage to God's plan. You will destroy this mission if you do not quit. You despise falseness yet you yourself are false because you are not holy enough to work so closely with God. Do not open your mouth and speak of God. If you do, you will be a hypocrite. God despises hypocrites and He will despise you. It would be better for your soul if you walked away from this mission right now. If you continue on, you will most certainly land in hell."

I fought the most severe temptation to walk off the stage and out of the room. Granted, there were team members who would have blocked my path and put me back up to open my mouth and allow the Lord to work but it must be noted that the consideration of altering my service was present.

I am saying that the Lord is not afraid of our temptations. He works nicely with us in spite of our difficulties. The Lord, in fact, allows these things so that we will always remember that He is God and we are not. We are God's servants and called to work in a spirit that is consistent with our Leader. Humility is everything.

What would be difficult for God is if we failed to present ourselves to Him for purifying. The good God cannot clean up our motives and inspirations if we do not place ourselves in His presence.

We must never be afraid that our temptations will separate us from God's service, as long as we take them to God. Bad inspirations will be eradicated through grace.

Protection Through Obedience

April 26, 2007

We, serving in our humanity, are subject to ups and downs. Our unique personalities present us with an infinite number of opportunities to become holy, to do battle against ourselves.

One could argue that our humanity creates vulnerability for God's plan, given that He has decided to flow through us and thus renew the face of the earth.

How do we protect God's plan? How do we protect the Lord's interests in our soul?

We protect God's plan through obedience. Obedience is the answer to the trouble in our times. Clearly, none of us can wave a magic wand and make everyone accept the holy spirit of obedience. God is not asking this. Instead, God gives us a realistic, manageable task, which is individually accepting the spirit of obedience in our own lives.

Oh my, how we struggle at times. If I am told not to answer emails for two months, I feel a magnetic pull to the computer. How many on an empty highway have not struggled to remain within the speed limit? I think that we each find opportunities to practice obedience and the spirit of obedience.

Clearly, if one thought that one would be caught speeding, one would reduce his speed and many of us have hit our breaks only after spotting a police officer pointing a radar gun. But isn't it better to drive within the speed limit simply out of respect for the laws written to protect us and other drivers?

Driving is an easy example so I will persist.

If we get into our cars to drive with a decision to be respectful of the law, we will complete each journey in greater calm. Breaking the law when driving causes stress and possible negative consequences, and, at worst, injury or even death. A decision to follow the rules takes the stress away, increases our safety and elevates the safety of the whole highway.

This is the same way in the spiritual life, our life in the Church. A decision to follow the rules in the Church removes a great deal of stress and limits the possible negative consequences in our souls, in our lives and also in the souls and lives of those around us. We must begin to see the guidance and direction of the Church as God-given for our protection, as opposed to man-given in order to control and stifle us.

I have heard it said that the Catholic Church is all about rules. Why is it that other faiths can have rules and it is viewed as acceptable but the Catholic Church's guidelines are seen as objectionable? Catholicism is, after all, a faith. The Church teaches us the way. There is intended an order and peace about the way we are taught to follow Jesus and treat each other. The guidelines we are asked to follow are not punitive, but protective in nature.

The Church is warning us, cautioning us, advising us and attempting to lead us. The Church is the vehicle through which God seeks to counsel His flock. Consider that if lambs rejected the shepherd, they would be lost and vulnerable. Should the lambs turn their back on their shepherd or react in rage when the shepherd draws them down a given path? Wouldn't it be ridiculous of the lambs to accuse the shepherd of stifling them? Controlling them? Wouldn't it be a foolish lamb that bites the shepherd when the shepherd tries to bring him to a safe place?

I am comparing us to lambs, as Jesus does, because we are vulnerable, as well as lovable.

If we reject the way, the direction that Jesus is giving us, we are at the mercy of the world and He cannot protect us.

A smart lamb, a thinking lamb would say to himself,

"Hmm. The shepherd knows what he is doing. He has been put in charge of this flock and no doubt knows the way home. It is in my best interest to follow Him and encourage others to follow Him so that we can all arrive home safely."

In each of our souls let us cultivate a spirit of obedience even as we accept and understand that our life today may not match the perfect obedience lived by Jesus.

In other words, we all accept that we can probably do a little bit better.

A lay apostle recently compared God to the best father on earth. This father will say, "Do not play in the street." If the child disobeys and is struck by a car, what will the good father do? The good father will rush to the wounded child at once, moving the child to safety and tending to his wounds. The good father could not possibly stand by while the child suffered, even though the child's suffering was the result of his disobedience.

Do Not Judge Others

March 27, 2007

How reverently the Lord views us. How perfect is His vision. Jesus Christ sees our condition with perfect clarity. Because the Lord is God and created us, He knows exactly what our life, lived in unity to the divine will, could and should look like. Jesus sees the beautiful potential in each of us. He sees the reality of the present condition of our soul and He sees the way our soul will look when it is completely united to Him, completely accepting of the divine will.

If we were to dwell on the distance between what we are today and what we could be if we were in perfect union with the divine will, we might become discouraged. I should remark that many of us do become discouraged. Certainly, each honest examination of conscience illuminates for us the distance we have yet to travel.

Is Jesus discouraged? No. I believe that Jesus is one who looks on the bright side when it comes to His apostles. I believe Jesus looks often at the distance behind us, in other words, the gains we have made in holiness. He then looks at where He would like us to go and prompts us in that direction. Jesus always encourages us to move further, to advance in holiness.

With regard to discouragement, each apostle should be committed to daily work in the soul, it is true, but with a respectful acceptance of the place in which he finds himself. If Jesus Christ has reverence for our process, our movement, our journey in holiness, so must we. We must be reverent of the fact that we are imperfect. We must be kind in the consideration of ourselves.

Does this mean accept our sinfulness? Yes and no. We accept that we are prone to sin. We reject that we are helpless against sinfulness.

The fact that we have sinned and will sin again should not inspire in us helplessness, but rather determination. The fact that we may fail Jesus today means that we must be on guard, not complacent. We must never lay down our sword when it comes to perfecting our behaviors and attitudes. If we want to become saints, and this is God's plan, the plan on which He has hinged the renewal, we must do battle daily for holiness. We must do battle daily for humility. We must do battle daily for detachment from our will and attachment to His will. People look at someone who evidences a high level of holiness and they think to themselves, If I were as holy as he is it would be easy.

This is the opposite of the truth. The holier one becomes, the more intense the battle, and the greater the necessity for vigilant struggle.

The opposite of this might be someone comparing himself to another and saying, "Thank God I am holier than that person." But how does he know where the other is doing battle? How does he know the place of departure in the holiness journey for another? Perhaps this person has made vast gains in holiness over time.

People must remember that the authentic struggle for holiness is completed in the privacy of the soul.

Holiness is not a competitive sport.

This process is between God and man, man and God. It is unseen to others and unavailable for scrutiny by a casual observer. I am keenly aware that I walk amongst apostles with extraordinary levels of holiness. Because I am aware of this, I feel God's reverence for others. I feel reverence for the place at which they are in their journey.

In an attempt to make this visual, let me propose that we

see a race being run. One participant, a trained athlete with near perfect physical ability, completes the mile race in 4 minutes. This is good, impressive, and we admire the athlete, especially if it is ourself.

Another runner is only a quarter of a mile along after twenty minutes. We think, This is not very impressive. That one is making no progress at all. He is hopeless in comparison. He'll never finish the race.

Perhaps, though, the slower one has handicaps that he is overcoming. Perhaps he has terrible pain in his hips. Perhaps he is blind and is having to feel his way along the course. Perhaps he is nearly paralyzed with fear that he will fail. Perhaps, in all of this, he has to proceed with the knowledge that others fly by him, seemingly far more equipped to be in the race than he is. Maybe he knows that others do not want him in the race because he doesn't seem to be running as fast as they are running. He feels unwelcome and unworthy. And yet he continues.

I ask you, who is working harder?

We are each a runner in this race. If God has allowed us to advance, we should give credit to God and run hard and constantly, understanding that we are called to work in a place different from anyone else. We should also understand that just as God has given us great opportunities for holiness, He could allow us to become handicapped at any time.

Making judgments against those we deem less holy than us will land us in a very bad, very unholy place. God will not countenance it forever. He cannot do so and still move us forward.

I am repeating the Lord's plea that we not judge others. We must not make decisions or pronouncements about the holiness or lack of holiness in another. If someone loves God, or even simply recognizes His dominion, rejoice. Rejoice in the goodness of each person you know. Pray that God advance each person you know. Help God to do so.

We must be constantly alert to any feelings of superiority we are harboring.

I feel the need to put even more clarity on this so let me give an example that, while limited, will perhaps point us in the right direction.

Compare two small boys. One is brought up by holy parents, surrounded by security and love. The other is brought up by one parent, as the other has left. Perhaps the remaining parent is badly wounded emotionally and addicted to drugs and alcohol. Additionally, this second boy is malnourished and never consistently receives what he needs in terms of security and parenting.

Could we make a fair comparison between the two before God has had time to heal the wounds of the second boy? Would God use the same measuring stick in either determining their holiness or assigning responsibilities? I don't think so.

Obviously, one has far more to overcome than the other. Jesus has provided for the second child to come into His service, perhaps through an apostle's love and acceptance of him. Perhaps the first boy is called to draw the second boy into the family of God. And then what?

He will fight his battles in the privacy of his soul, wherein he will find his healing. Usually, this healing will be a process. It will not happen overnight, but gradually, slowly, gently, perhaps assisted by our compassionate acceptance of where he comes from, where he is at today and where he is called to go tomorrow.

We cannot call people back into our family and then object because they do not become saints overnight.

When people come back to God's Church in great numbers, and they will, we must be prepared to accept them as Jesus accepts them, wounds and all.

The wounds will heal with time and love.

There can be an unfortunate message sent by some that communicates, "We do not want you messy." The reality is, though, God accepts us in any condition. We must accept others in the same spirit.

A lovely apostle was talking to another woman. The woman's daughter was a recovering drug addict with two children and an absent father. She had recently returned to the Church.

The woman sighed heavily and said, "She's a bit of a disaster."

The apostle replied with loving indignation.

"You are so wrong. Your daughter is a triumph for each one of us. The whole family of God is blessed because she has returned to us. We badly needed her so we must do everything we can to help her in these early days of her return."

This filled the mother with joy and that, my friends, is the correct spirit.

It will be good if we can all be aware that each of those around us is somewhere in the process of perfection. We must be acutely aware of God's project in each soul, in each other, and respect that God is moving as quickly as He can. Also, we want to be certain that we contribute to God's process in each soul and not detract from God's effort.

Consider how an aid worker treats a person who is starving and in serious condition through being deprived of nourishment over time. The aid worker does not offer this person rich foods in great quantity. The starvation victim would be unable to tolerate rich foods in great quantity. The aid worker gently offers little bits of nourishment, often and regularly. In this way the starvation victim is not overcome.

The aid worker knows that if he offered a magnificent dinner with steak, potatoes, vegetables, breads and ice creams, the starvation victim would be overwhelmed. To expect the starvation victim to either ingest it all at once or recover immediately after one meal is unrealistic. Such an expectation would correctly be considered ridiculous.

When we look to those around us who are away from the Church, away from Christ and things that are heavenly, we must consider them the same way. Let us have an optimal expectation, of course, because we would never be wise to limit God's power and influence, but let us be acutely aware of the gradual nature of most conversions.

If someone has been away from God for some time, feed them small bits of simple truths.

Do not begin with "You are a sinner."

We are each sinners and we must all be assured that most souls away from God are aware of their condition.

We are not called to be the sin police. We are called to be the deliverers of God's love.

Instead we must give heavenly sustenance in small doses wrapped in simple packages. Jesus loves you. Jesus is with you. Jesus will heal you. Jesus will come for you one day. Jesus will protect His interests in your soul if you allow Him to do so.

Also, it is a snare to place an expectation on the recipient of the love we bring. We think, I have brought you this nourishment. I know it to be good. Why don't you take it and walk like me or walk in the manner I believe is holy?

We can be tempted to get frustrated with the recipient because he does not advance fast enough or because he backslides at times. We are tempted to treat each person moving slowly as a personal failure. We have all experienced this or seen it in others.

How do we deliver God's Good News?

We must be very reverent with people.

Consider a man. He loves God. He knows God is good. This man is Catholic, but not always practicing. Still, he recognizes the authority of the Church.

Is he getting it wrong to have sex with his fiancé? Yes. Of course he is.

Is he making a mistake by drinking too much at times? Yes. That's a mistake.

Is he offending God by taking His name in vain? Certainly.

What is the most important thing in God's Kingdom? Love.

How does this man treat others? Respectfully and with love.

Does this man judge others? No. He is known to be kind and generous and charitable.

I do not know where God is taking him. I am not on his path. I am on my path and I must concentrate on where God wants me to go, leaving this man's process to him.

I believe it is important to correct those in error as people have at times corrected me. But we must do so gently, usually with one sentence and then leave it with them. We must speak with the understanding that God sees the whole person, not just the sin. God looks at everyone and rejoices in goodness, even while His light identifies areas where change is necessary.

Which one of us would deny that our past pain from our sins has given us wisdom and compassion?

Do not judge others. Bring others God's love and God's truth.

May 16, 2007

Yes, it is truth that each of us is involved in a process and the movement to obedience for each of us is a process, a gradual turning of our hearts and minds completely to the Father's will. In heaven, we will be so beautiful because we will be fully united with the divine will. How joyous an expectation this is for each of us.

In this time, there are many away from the Father's intended plan for them. I say this because it is true. I believe that lay apostles, to be pleasing to Christ and to be like Christ, must look at brothers and sisters living in error differently. We must do away with the mathematical-like evaluation system designed by humanity that ends with, "They are not as holy as we are."

Jesus sees each person and rejoices in the potential, as I have said. He sees what the soul will look like when it has allowed itself to be fully united to the divine will. This gives Jesus hope, even while He feels grief at the pain of the person who has rejected the divine will. The fruits of disobedience are shame and sadness, after all, and these are heavy burdens. So while Jesus is aware of the wounds, He is optimistic about the future of each person.

Jesus is accepting because He knows us so well and He loves us so much. Jesus is optimistic because he has watched so many conversions. The Lord understands that there is no sinful condition that cannot be rectified by repentance. He waits patiently for the time of repentance to come.

We are called to be gentle with all others because we do not know their whole story, even if they are our family members. Jesus knows their whole story. He sees the big picture. He will see to them and He will help us to discern the best way to love each person He places in our life.

Please be patient with this writer who repeats herself. I do so because I believe that the greatest enemy to the conversion of many is the lack of love offered by believers. We must not place the heavy burden of our human judgment on a soul trembling with the desire to return to God. Surely that soul would be deterred by our limited understanding of God's mercy.

I will venture even further. Look at a soul whom you believe to be living in error. Perhaps you know of someone who is living with another in a presumably sexual way without benefit of marriage. Perhaps you know someone who is involved in a homosexual lifestyle. Many hasten to make judgments about the condition of these souls. While the Church identifies objective states of grave sin, it is not our task to determine the state of another's soul.

Jesus looks at them and sees the sin of those in error, of course, and perhaps Jesus sees that they rebel against Him personally, if in fact they do, but Jesus sees something else. Jesus sees any respect they have for others. Jesus sees any warmth or compassion in them. He sees the kindness practiced by each soul in every day. He sees their yearning for Him and for purity and goodness. Jesus waits, hoping that His apostles will set an example of love and acceptance that will draw others.

To be clear, Jesus rejects the sin of impure sexual actions and He rejects the sin of behaving cruelly and judgmentally in His name. I wonder which would offend Him most.

Jesus rejects sin, not people.

We must look constantly for the goodness in each of the souls around us. We must take that goodness and offer it to Jesus, asking Him to help that goodness to grow so that each soul can be aware of the path to greater holiness. Jesus rebuked the Pharisees for laying heavy burdens on people and making no move to lift them. I believe that we do this when we make sweeping statements of a condemning nature about those we believe are in a state of sin.

In other words, we must accept that a Catholic person's return to the Church is not always an overnight phenomenon. I have seen it take a long time. St. Monica prayed for her son, St. Augustine, for years before he converted. When he did return, he certainly left a mark. Others will, too.

When we speak to people living in a state of rebellion against the Church, perhaps, if welcomed to do so, we should help them to identify manageable course corrections. I have spoken in other places about a person departing from the true course by one degree. We said that the departure does not look alarming on the first day, or even after the first week, but by the first year we will surely see a distance between the correct course and the course of the one who departed by one degree in the past.

In the same way, if we help someone to adjust their far off course by one degree, their condition will not look starkly different on the first day, or even after the first week, but by the first year after a course alteration, regardless of how small, we will surely be able to identify that they have in some way closed the distance between the place of error and the place of the divine will.

We must accept that from the outside, a person's situation may not appear to be changing. But maybe on the inside, God has brought the person a great deal closer to Him or even brought the person closer to a moment of life-altering grace that will convert the individual instantaneously. We simply do not know and we have to accept that we do not know, and, as previously stated, be reverent in the presence of God's on-going project in others.

Souls are returning. We must be patient as Christ is patient.

Part Three

Snapshots of Reality

The following are brief fictional illustrations of how Jesus teaches us to love in our daily lives.

A Long Day

Father Matthew struck out at the ringing alarm clock. It did not turn off. He swung his arm out again, landing expertly on the snooze button. Still the assault on his sleep continued. His mind cleared the smallest bit and Father Matthew registered that it was the telephone, not the alarm that dragged him so cruelly from his rest.

"Yes? Yes?" he muttered into the phone.

"Father, is that you?" a man asked. The urgency in the man's voice ripped the cobwebs from his mind and the priest rose onto one elbow.

"Yes, I'm here. What is it?"

"It's Gerry Cauffield, Father. My mother is very sick. She…I think she's dying."

"Right. Are you at home, Gerry?"

"I am, Father. The doctor is coming. She's afraid. There's something bothering her."

"Fine, Gerry. I'll be over. I'll be right there."

Father Matthew hung up the phone and stared stupidly at the wall. It was 2:00 a.m. He had been at a parish council meeting refereeing a battle over refreshments for the Spring Festival until 11:00 p.m. Sleep had eluded him until well after midnight.

"Where are my pants?" he mumbled aloud as he swung his feet onto the floor.

Moments later he pulled his jacket around himself and stepped out into a cold night. Revellers congregated in the street as the bars ejected the last of their patrons. They did not seem to feel the cold, Matthew thought, but then they had not come into the night from a warm bed. Matthew drove past them, trying to force himself to focus on the job at hand.

Mrs. Caufield, a widow, had cancer. When he visited her the previous week, she had appeared to be holding her own. Father Matthew had sensed that something was bothering the woman but he could hardly demand that she be forthcoming about it. He felt indebted to Mrs. Caufield as she had been a solid support to him when he first arrived in the parish. Yes, he mused, many felt gratitude to her for kind acts and compassion. She lived her faith, he decided.

On this night, the house was lit from every corner, in contrast to the darkened houses nearby. Nobody slept in this home, he thought as he pulled into the driveway.

Gerry held open the door for him and the look on the man's face put speed into his steps.

"Thank you, Father. She's very distressed."

Father Matthew followed the hallway down into the sick room. The face of death greeted him and Father Matthew felt a calm purpose come over him. His sleepiness vanished.

Mrs. Caufield lay upright, propped against a stack of pillows. As he often saw in cases of death, it seemed as if her face wanted to melt into the pillow and become part of it. Her eyes were closed but they were not shut in a peaceful way. He could see constant wincing and agitation.

"Mrs. Caufield, it's Father Matthew," he said loudly.

The woman's arm flailed out at the air beside the bed and Father Matthew quickly stepped next to her, catching her bony hand in his own.

"I'm here," he said quietly. "I'm going to anoint you."

"Father," she cried out pitifully. "Help me. I can't die. I won't be welcome in heaven. Jesus hates me."

Her son's face betrayed his anxiety. "She's been saying that all evening, Father. I don't know a better woman then my mother. It's not right. She keeps crying."

Father Matthew nodded. "Leave me with her for a moment, Gerry. It'll be all right. She just wants a chat."

Gerry nodded with gratitude and backed out of the room.

"Sarah," Father Matthew said, "Would you like me to hear your Confession?"

The patient's eyes opened the smallest bit and he saw tears leaking from the sides. "I don't think God will forgive me, Father. I've carried this sin for a long time."

Father Matthew kept hold of the little hand and used his foot to pull at the leg of a chair, moving it up close to the top of the bed. "Time to get rid of it, Sarah. God will forgive you. Tell me what's bothering you so I can help. You wanted to tell me last week, I think."

Mrs. Caufield, breathless, opened her eyes more fully and focused on the priest's face.

"I did," she said softly. "But I couldn't. Now I'm dying. Father, does God forgive murder? I need to know and then you can tell me if there's any point in Confession."

"He does indeed, Sarah. God forgives any sin if a sinner repents."

The woman closed her eyes to rest. Father Matthew remained quiet. Soon she opened her eyes again and began to speak.

"My daughter Lorretta was so beautiful," she said weakly. "We loved her so much. She was academically...you didn't know her...she was gifted."

Father Matthew stayed still.

"She had plans to be a doctor. Father, I was so proud. Her father was so proud. She was going to be a wonderful doctor." A sound came from the woman's throat and she began to choke, coughing and sputtering. Matthew pulled the cloth from her chest to her mouth and held her head as she recovered. Afterward, Sarah Caufield lay back on her pillow again, exhausted. Father Matthew waited and soon enough, she continued.

"At the end of her second year at university, she came home for a weekend. I knew something was not right. She looked worried. A mother knows and I sensed there was something. On Sunday she told me she was pregnant. There was a boy there, you see, and she was dating him, but pregnant? I'll never forget it. I wanted to die."

Sarah stared past Father Matthew with eyes that looked upon another scene.

"She wanted to have the baby, Father. She said she loved this boy. He was in school as well. I couldn't bear it. I…it would have killed her father. I talked her out of it and went with her to have an abortion."

Matthew, aware of his facial features, did not hesitate. "Are you sorry, Sarah?"

She began to weep. "I've spent every day in hell since. Lorretta became a doctor, but she never really smiled again. She broke up with that boy. Then she died in the car accident. Father Matthew," she wept, "Lorretta was only twenty-eight when she died. And she died with a broken heart because she missed her baby. I know this is true and it's my fault. After she died my husband kept saying 'If only she had had a child we'd have some part of her.' I never told him. How could I? I think, if I'm honest, he would have accepted the baby. He didn't care what people thought. I did, Father, and I allowed my grandchild, his grandchild, to be killed. How could Jesus forgive that?"

Sarah leaned forward in grief, nearly falling, and Father Matthew caught her into his arms. She wept weakly, as much as her condition allowed. The priest prayed with his whole heart, understanding once again the truth about sorrow.

"Sarah," Father Matthew said firmly, "Have you told Jesus that you're sorry?"

Sarah nodded against him. "I've told Jesus I'm sorry every

day since. I was wrong. I had no courage. I see so many who have babies like this and they cope. We would have coped. The baby would be nearly grown now."

Sarah's head turned back and forth jerkily, as if Mrs. Caufield sought to escape from the terrible remorse.

"Listen to me, Sarah."

The insistence in his voice stopped her movements and she listened, eyes open, concentrating intently on his face. Father Matthew felt the grace in the room and understood that the authority coming from him was not his own.

"Jesus forgave you for this sin a long time ago. Jesus is asking you to accept His forgiveness. Do you trust Jesus?"

"I do," she cried. "I do."

"Then accept this gift, the gift of His forgiveness. Loretta is with her child and with your husband. Everything is all right. Your grandchild is in heaven and they are all waiting for you. All is forgiven, Sarah. They are praying for peace for you and Jesus is answering their prayer. Accept God's grace and through your acceptance of this grace, God will bless your son, who has to go on living."

Father Matthew felt peace flowing through him into the dying woman, and he watched as she relaxed. He laid her back gently into the pillows.

Sarah rested for a moment. Father Matthew felt relief as he observed the altered countenance of her features. No longer did she squint and wince.

"Sarah," Father Matthew said softly, "You were a good mother to your children. You did years of volunteer work with the mentally ill. Do you have any idea how many people you helped there alone? Do you think God forgets this? Remember how you helped me when I arrived? I would not have been able to stick with it here if you hadn't supported me. You made a mistake, Sarah. Others have made the same mistake only you don't know about them. God sees all the good you've done, all the kindness you've given to people. Trust me, Sarah. God loves you and He has forgiven you."

After a moment, she opened her eyes.

"Father," she said with dignity. "Will you hear my Confession?"

A few hours later, ringing dragged Father Matthew from yet another inadequate rest. This time it was the alarm and he successfully aimed for and achieved the snooze button. He tried to fall back into the precious ten minutes but it was too late. His brain began to replay the night's events.

Sarah Caufield had died peacefully, in a death that seemed to fill the room and all in it with grace. Thank God, he thought, marvelling at the pain she had carried for so long.

His mind backed up past the middle of the night deathbed and into the parish council meeting. He groaned and pulled a second pillow over his head. Two dedicated volunteers had adopted opposing positions on whether or not to serve refreshments after the music recital. One woman insisted the refreshments be served at the intermission; another insisted that the refreshments be served afterward. Father Matthew had listened, along with the rest of the committee, to lengthy arguments from both, finally ending the discussion by citing the lateness of the hour. He noted as he darted out to his car after the meeting that each of the women had attracted small groups of sympathetic committee members.

Sides had been established. He anticipated the second exchange after the morning Mass.

Bleary eyed, Father Matthew rose and began to dress, saying the Allegiance Prayer.

After Mass, Father Matthew removed his vestments in the sacristy. He had prayed for patience and humility. His mind struggled to focus and Father Matthew decided that fatigue could actually be an aid to holiness given that he could not remain long enough on any one thought to feel annoyance.

These two women made The Standoff an annual event, as predictable as the first flowers in spring. Last night Father Matthew had felt a certain amount of ire. Today he was too tired to care. It would be an easy thing if the women were not holy, dedicated parishioners. But both served tirelessly in the parish and Father Matthew needed them both and felt great affection for them both. They were loyal and he appreciated it. They simply could not get along.

"Father?" said a small, sweet voice.

Father Matthew, head in his robe, turned toward the voice. "Yes? I'm here."

"Father, do you have a minute?"

Day two, round one.

"It's very important that we settle this decision so the refreshments committee can proceed. I think Sandra means well but she has no understanding of the facility."

"Yes, of course. Ask Sandra to come in and we'll fight it…uh, sort it out."

Thirty minutes later, Father Matthew looked at his watch in relief. Mercifully, he had to go. It wasn't a lie or excuse. He had to be at the school for Confessions in thirty minutes. That left fifteen minutes to eat breakfast and fifteen to travel. Suppressing a large yawn, he tried to look intelligent while he wondered what kept these two busy in the fall. There were no autumn festivals. Hmm. The connecting parish had an autumn festival. Had that been last year or two years ago? Last year was the big rain so it would have been indoors….

"Father," snapped Sandra. "Are you in the room at all?"

Had his eyes been closed? "Help me, Jesus," he prayed.

"I was just thinking how well it went last year when the two of you handled the decorations," he said soothingly, not missing a beat. "You know, many people said they had never seen more dramatic sets for a musical performance. It is amazing to me what you two can do when you team up. I mean, I was really impressed."

Matthew, barely aware of what he was saying, saw with relief that the women appeared mollified. Last year's achievement had tested all of Father Matthew's diplomatic skills. He had seen an advertisement for the Oscars on television yesterday. That must be where the term musical performance had come from.

The two exchanged smiles, remembering their shared success. Matthew pushed his advantage.

"I am certain," he spoke, rising, "that I can leave this decision and all of these arrangements in your hands." He said this in a chatty tone as he pulled his coat on and opened the door. "That's how much I trust you both. I'm due over at the school for Confessions. Look at the sunshine," he continued talking, walking. Keep moving toward the car, he thought. Look like you're hurrying, stare straight ahead.

They would have to work it out.

One night of missing sleep did not affect him too much but this was two in a row and Father Matthew yawned deeply as he drove. He had Confessions until 1pm and then a vocations talk at the high school. After that he had to attend a meeting for the education committee. He thought wistfully about taking a nap but knew it would not happen. He would be needed at the Caufield's and he had a couple coming in for their wedding rehearsal that evening. That would be a golden opportunity for practicing patience.

All at once, he felt very tired. He yawned again.

Hearing the Confessions of nine-year-olds restored his spiritual buoyancy. Father Matthew marvelled at the depth of spirituality in children. Before he left he gave the class a talk on the Eucharist.

A child raised her hand. "Father," she asked, ignoring the subject at hand, "are you married? Do you have kids?"

"No," he replied.

"Why do we call you Father? Are you like God the Father or are you like human fathers?"

"Well, I work for God. You call priests Father because God, who is everyone's father, works through them."

"Are we talking about Jesus or God?"

Father Matthew prayed for guidance. They were heading for a discussion of the Trinity. "We're talking about Jesus and God the Father as well as the Holy Spirit, Terri. All three are the same God."

She rolled her eyes. "Right. It's like the shamrock. But if you're not married, who cooks your dinner?"

"Uh, I cook my dinner," he answered. "Sometimes I eat out."

A boy raised his hand. "Who washes your clothes?"

Terri answered for him. "He washes his own clothes. Who do you think washes his clothes?"

"Do you make your own bed?" persisted the boy.

"Yes. I make my own bed."

Another boy raised his hand. "Who do you watch television with at night?"

Matthew considered. "If I'm at home and I am watching television, I watch it by myself."

There was silence as they digested this. Another girl raised her hand. "Father, maybe you should get a dog. My uncle watches television alone. He's not married either but he doesn't work for God. He works for the electric company. He has a dog. The dog likes Power Rangers and the News but my uncle doesn't watch Power Rangers so I turn it on for the dog when I am there and the dog watches it with me. If you got a dog, he would watch television with you.

"That's a very good idea," Father Matthew said thoughtfully. "I'll think about that. Now be sure to say your prayers and I'll see you all at Mass on Sunday."

A little girl raised her hand urgently.

"Okay, one more question," Father Matthew said.

"Father, you better not get the dog. Who would watch it when you said Mass on Sunday?"

"That's a good point, Marie. I hadn't thought of that."

"And what about during the week? Who would watch the dog during the week?" asked another boy.

At this point the teacher rose from her seat in the back of the room and reclaimed the class. "Father only works on weekends, Sean. He's off during the week but let's leave the decision of the dog with him. Thank you for coming in, Father. What do we say, class?"

"Thank you, Father Matthew," they intoned.

Father Matthew left, bristling with indignation. What did she mean he was off during the week? He only worked weekends? That was news to him. Why would she say such a thing? Did she think that hearing fifty Confessions was being off? Or sitting in on these meetings? Or making peace constantly between warring parties or getting up and facing the most definitive moments of people's lives with them was being off? He felt his anger bubbling and snapped himself back.

Why did it bother him so much? That was the more important question. God never guaranteed him he would be appreciated by those he served. Father Matthew tried to let it go as he made his way to the talk on vocations. He cheered himself up by thinking about lunch.

"Father," asked one of the fifteen-year-olds. "Does it bother you that so many priests are pedophiles?"

Father Matthew prayed silently to the Holy Spirit for inspiration. "Yes," he answered quietly. "It bothers me terribly that any person would molest another person and it bothers me even more terribly when it is a priest who commits this crime."

Forty-five silent faces looked at him. He was glad it came up. He should rejoice, actually, because recent disclosures in the press had shaken up the whole region. This was a part of his ministry, he knew, to serve in this time of distress for the Church. He reminded God that he was there to speak for Him.

"I believe that the men who behaved this way betrayed the people they were supposed to serve and I believe they betrayed God, too. I think God is very hurt by this and I think that it is God who is bringing this all out into the open so that it cannot happen again. At the end of our talk, we'll pray for all people who have been molested by anyone but especially, let's pray for all people who have been molested by priests because it makes it very difficult for them to trust other priests."

He saw a few nod their heads in agreement and he moved on.

"This is part of the reason we need more vocations. We need brave men and women to bring all that is good about the priesthood and religious life to others. Think of it this way. If you were a priest or a nun, you would not behave this way. People who met you would recognize God's goodness in you and you would be able to help them. That's what I want to do. I want to help people so that they can know God and know that God loves them."

Matthew went on to talk about the various types of vocations and finished the talk peacefully. As he left the school, he felt dejected. Vocations had all but dried up in the diocese and the comment from the student had been bitter and accusatory. Whatever, he thought. It was time for lunch.

"Father," called a voice. He turned and saw an earnest looking student following him. The young man was tall and looked like he had not yet grown accustomed to his long legs and arms.

"Yes?" Father Matthew answered.

The boy looked embarrassed. "I just wanted to say thank you."

Matthew felt a rise of emotion, possibly gratitude. "You're welcome. What's your name?"

"My name is Farrell. My uncle is a priest in Africa."

"That's wonderful, Farrell."

"My uncle is a great guy," Farrell noted. "I have to go or I'll be late for class. I just think it was good you answered that question the way you did. Thanks again."

Farrell took off with a wave.

Father Matthew stood for a moment looking after him. "Thank *you*, Farrell," he said to himself.

He then drove off cheerfully in search of lunch. He would need to fuel himself for the education committee.

The Bathrobe

Theresa rose slowly, stretching as she assessed the morning's pain. Mornings brought stiffness which sometimes dissipated as the day wore on. Not too bad this morning. She thanked God.

The kettle began to hum as she rinsed the few dishes in the sink and prepared a light breakfast. When the table was laid with oatmeal and toast, she poured a cup of tea and let it brew. Theresa sat down, making the Sign of the Cross. She thanked God for her breakfast and then said the Morning Offering and the Allegiance Prayer, giving God her life, work, and heart. She offered brief prayers for her deceased husband and two grown children and ate her breakfast, considering the day ahead.

Nursing elderly patients brought many opportunities to practice patience and Theresa asked Jesus to give her extra patience on this day. One of the women in her care was given to angry outbursts that caused great upset amongst the staff. This woman continually told this one about that one, stirring up trouble.

"Jesus, protect us from her," Theresa prayed. "Help me to keep my own temper and be kind to Mrs. Lambert, even if she behaves terribly."

The elderly Mrs. Lambert had only been in care for a short time. A widow, Mrs. Lambert had three grown children.

God help them, Theresa thought idly.

Theresa thought of her lay apostle commitment and resolved to treat the troubled Mrs. Lambert with the kindness of Jesus Christ.

"Lord," she prayed, "This will have to come from you. Put Your love in my heart for this woman and help me to see You in her. Help me to say exactly what she needs to hear today and let her feel Your love in my presence. Jesus, help me to forgive her for lying about me yesterday."

Satisfied that she had put the problem in the right place, Theresa finished her breakfast and began clearing the few dishes. Yesterday had been difficult in the extreme because Mrs. Lambert told another nurse that Theresa had complained about her. An ugly confrontation resulted, leaving Theresa shaken and nearly in tears. After she calmed herself, Theresa had returned to the other nurse, Terri, and the two had straightened it out, correctly identifying Mrs. Lambert as the source of the problem. Theresa shook her head as she rinsed the dishes. Imagine if she had left it alone. She could not have slept with the upset of it. Given what Mrs. Lambert had told Terri, Terri's reaction was understandable. Once the truth was revealed, Theresa and Terri felt peaceful toward each other and resolved to check any of Mrs. Lambert's statements against the truth.

Thank God, Theresa thought again. Work was difficult enough without someone angry at you or ignoring you.

Theresa parked her car and unbuckled her seat belt. The pain in her hands made it difficult and she offered the pain to God, along with a prayer for healing. Theresa was beginning an experimental drug for arthritis and she hoped that God would heal her through it.

"Take the suffering if you can, Lord," she prayed. "I'm worn out with it."

The lights of the nursing home radiated cheerfulness in the winter morning's dimness and Theresa felt peace as she greeted others. Mrs. Lambert's room was last on her morning round. Theresa always dreaded the interactions.

"Good morning, Mrs. Lambert," she said serenely as she carried her tray into the elderly woman's room. "Time for bloods."

"Is there nobody else who can take my blood?" the old woman asked angrily. "You've got me stabbed to death."

Mrs. Lambert's illness resulted in increased bruising. Theresa knew that it was not her fault that the elderly woman bruised but Mrs. Lambert told everyone who would listen that Theresa deliberately hurt her.

Theresa considered her patient for a moment. Mrs. Lambert's perpetual frown caused her eyes to nearly disappear in her face. When Theresa did meet her eyes, she was met with snapping anger and bitterness. Shrunken in body, the elderly woman looked tiny in the bed. She wore a large green bathrobe that she kept wrapped tightly around her. It was ugly, Theresa observed, and worn out. There were at least three new ones in her bedside locker, brought by her children, but Mrs. Lambert refused to wear any other.

Glancing sideways at her, Theresa felt a rush of unusual compassion for her querulous patient. She glanced at Mrs. Lambert again, surprised, and felt another wave of pity wash over her. She thought of Jesus and how He must view this woman.

"God help you, Mrs. Lambert, it's not easy being in here."

The words burst from Theresa unexpectedly. The level of compassion and mercy she felt nearly doubled her over as she gazed on the emaciated woman. Mrs. Lambert, instead of snapping back something hateful, frowned even deeper but remained silent.

Encouraged by the surprising love she felt for her patient, Theresa continued speaking. It was as if God's mercy washed into the room in waves.

"Your bathrobe looks so comfortable and warm. You must love being wrapped up in it." Theresa continued speaking, soothingly, softly, as she drew blood, expecting the silence to end at any second with a biting reproach.

I'm getting some of God's kindness into her anyway, Theresa thought, encouraged. Mrs. Lambert pulled her bathrobe sleeve down over her arm when Theresa finished, wrapping the robe even more tightly around herself. She glanced furtively at Theresa, but remained silent.

"I'll be in later," Theresa said cheerfully, picking up her tray. "God bless."

In the employee break room, Terri handed her a cup of coffee.

"How is the she-devil today?"

Theresa frowned. "She's the same, I guess. I don't know. She started by demanding someone else to draw her blood."

Terri's eyes danced. "You wouldn't want to trip and stick her in the eye, Theresa. Be careful."

Theresa laughed in spite of herself. "You're rotten, Terri. What a thing to say."

"Sorry," Terri said, a little ashamed. "I didn't get much sleep last night."

"She's warming up I think. I'm praying so hard for her and I'm starting to feel sorry for her."

Terri looked at her friend thoughtfully. "Well, it's a bit like feeling sorry for a rattlesnake but I'll pray too and we'll shoot for some emotional healing. It'll have to be a miracle."

Theresa nodded. It certainly would.

Later, Theresa steeled herself, said a quick prayer to St. Michael, and headed back into the room.

"Me, again," she said cheerfully.

Mrs. Lambert extended her arm silently, pulling up her sleeve. Theresa remained quiet, praying.

"My husband worked for the phone company," Mrs. Lambert snapped out. "Thirty years. He retired young and then started a business building fences. He came home for dinner every night. He wasn't sick a day in his life."

Theresa kept working. "That was wonderful for him."

Silence.

"He was a good husband," Mrs. Lambert said. Theresa listened to her voice. It was as if Mrs. Lambert was unaccustomed to conversing anymore. The woman clearly had to work to keep her tone conversational, instead of accusatory.

"Yes, he was a good man. A funny man. Louis could always make me laugh."

Theresa nodded, trying to picture something like laughter coming from this little package of hostility.

"We sure had fun. I took good care of him. He always had his meals ready when he came home, his laundry done. When the children grew up and left, we had each other. It was nice."

"How long since he died, Mrs. Lambert?"

There was no response and Theresa looked up to see Mrs. Lambert's face working. Dear Jesus, she thought, she's crying.

Finished taking blood, Theresa sat still with her hand on the elderly woman's arm. She prayed while Mrs. Lambert cried, sitting in silence.

"You miss him terribly," Theresa observed.

With this, Mrs. Lambert leaned her head forward and sobbed aloud. Theresa sat.

After some time, Mrs. Lambert raised her head. Theresa handed her a box of tissues.

"He bought me this bathrobe right before he died," she said. "It was Mother's Day and my two girls were coming over with their children. He gave it to me before they came and said, 'Mrs., open it now before they come.' Green is my favorite color." She looked at Theresa with eyes filled with pain. "I wanted to die first. I can't live without him." The last sentence was spoken in puzzlement, like a child. "He was old but we didn't have any health problems. He just died that night. It was so sudden. If I could have nursed him maybe I would have been ready. I would have done anything for him. Right after that, I had a stroke. Now cancer." Her eyes pleaded with Theresa for understanding. "Do you see? Six months ago I was in my home with Daniel and our two dogs. Now…I…there's nothing left."

Theresa listened and sympathized, praying, praying, and praying. She begged for God's grace and thanked God for His mercy for this woman. Theresa thanked God again and again for helping her to be kind and not judgmental of poor suffering Mrs. Lambert.

The Fire Chief

"Stop. STOP," Angela shrieked as her three-year-old sprayed the kitchen hose across the kitchen at the stove. She should have known when he got into the sink for his bath wearing nothing but his fireman helmet that he had a plan.

The flame under the pot of soup sizzled and went out.

"YES!" little John shouted. "I'm a real fire man,"

"Help me, God," she prayed.

Angela took the kitchen hose from his hand, replacing it before she put the burner knob to the off position.

"No, John. No more hose."

The doorbell rang.

"Come in," she yelled.

It rang again and she heard her eighteen-month-old knocking on the door from the inside.

"Come in. Come in. Come in," babbled the baby.

With a sigh of exasperation Angela pulled her son from the sink into a towel. He began to shout in protest with deafening shrieks in her face as she made her way to the door. Through the glass window she saw her father. Why didn't he just come in, she thought in frustration. She moved her toddler gently away from the door with her leg and saw that one of the children had locked it. Angela unlocked it and admitted her father.

"Good morning," he said cheerfully. In his early sixties, Angela's father was active and helpful. "How are the babies?"

"Grandpa, Grandpa," little Martina sang, clapping her hands. Grandpa pulled her up into his arms and surveyed the house. Dirty diapers, wipes, diaper cream and dirty pajamas sat on the table. A roll of toilet paper had been unrolled and strewn through the living room. Every book from the bookshelf lay on the floor and the breakfast dishes remained on the table.

"Tough morning?" he asked his twenty-eight-year-old daughter. Angela, still in pajamas, had her hair pulled up into a pony tail.

"You could say that," she replied. "I can't seem to get ahead of them. I get one thing cleaned up and they're three messes ahead. I'm not shooting for extraordinary here, Dad. I just want to get us all dressed by noon."

He followed her into the kitchen carrying Martina. He spotted the water mess from the hose.

"You need to let me disconnect that hose," he observed. The hose was a constant source of disaster in the home.

Angela put her son back into the sink, which stopped the shrieks. "No, Dad. I like the hose. They should learn not to play with it."

"Whatever you say, Honey. It just seems like they can't handle the temptation. I mean, he's wearing the Fire Chief's hat, he has a hose and there's a fire within fifteen feet of him. I might have put it out myself if I was standing naked in the sink wearing that hat."

"Well, I can't remove everything," she snapped. "They should learn to listen."

Grandpa distracted himself by playing with the little girl on his hip, who grabbed his hat from his head and put it back on, delighted with his howls of protest.

Angela took a washcloth and began to scrub the diaper cream from her son's face and abdomen, where he had smeared it while she dressed his sister. She fought tears of frustration.

"I don't think I'm doing so well, Dad."

"Why not?" he asked putting his granddaughter up over his head. This created noise as she giggled but his field of vision was clear to look at his daughter.

"I'm barely getting by. The house is only clean for two hours at night. That's on a good day and that's not floors and bathrooms. That just means you can walk through the living room. Going to the grocery store is like a nightmare with these two. Dan is never…I repeat, never here. I may as well be as single parent. I never pray anymore."

Her father looked on with compassion. "You're praying right now. Washing that child is prayer. God doesn't expect anything more from you, Angela. He's grateful for what you're doing."

Angela considered. "I seem to be yelling at them a lot."

"Yes, well, they're sociopaths," he joked, swinging Martina through the air with a whooshing sound, which produced squeals of laughter. "Look at it this way. When you clean up that wet toilet paper mess in the living room, it'll be like saying a Hail Mary. When you scrub the diaper rash cream off the wall…"

"What wall?"

Her father grimaced. "You didn't find that yet? Sorry. It's not too bad and its wallpaper. It'll come off…when you clean that off it's like an Our Father. You could put a whole Rosary together in these two rooms alone."

She laughed. "John was up throwing up all night. I haven't even gotten to the sheets and blankets."

"That's equivalent to a whole Mass, I think, depending on the amount of sleep loss. Angela, don't worry that you're not praying enough when you're taking care of these kids. Every day you get up and slap order on this house, remaining in any way cheerful, you give God a great gift. Going to Mass or saying the Rosary is easy compared to this gig. Your mother used to say one-sentence prayers all day long."

Heartened, Angela smiled. That was another way to look at it.

"Dan is never here, Dad. He's working constantly."

"Why?"

"He's working on a special project. No more money, of course, just more hours."

Grandpa put Martina up in the air again.

"He can't help it," his daughter continued taking off the Fire Chief's hat to shampoo her son. "I'm trying not to be mad about it but then he's tired when he gets home. To clarify, he's not too tired to play basketball on Wednesdays, and he always seems to get away in time for that. It just seems so unfair. Look at my life. His hasn't changed at all. I haven't got a coherent thought in my head. I'm starting to talk like these kids."

"It passes," her father said thoughtfully. "It really does. It seems unfair because you're home all the time and nobody is giving you a paycheck. The only one who really knows what your day looks like is God."

"That's for sure," she agreed. "I get no credit around here."

"Dress that boy and then you go over to Church for an hour. I'll stay here."

"Are you sure?" she asked. "Are you up for it?"

"Sure. I'm not due anywhere. Stop for groceries if you want."

"Dad," she said cheering considerably. "You're great. I'll be fast. I promise."

"No problem."

Exactly six minutes later, Angela raced out the door. As an experienced mother, she knew that any opportunity to get off alone was an opportunity to be seized as quickly as possible. The days were so long, she mused. There was simply no relief.

She drove, thinking. Her life consisted of the same messes, the same fights, over and over. She always thought she would be a happy mother but she had never guessed it would be this hard. Maybe it was her. Maybe she was the problem.

She pulled into the church parking lot feeling weary and discouraged. She really didn't even feel like praying. She would rather go to the mall. She thought of her father and sighed again, discouraged even more by her lack of holiness. The least she could do was go light a candle.

Angela knelt down in the pew and prayed. "God, give me a desire to pray. It's like I've lost the habit altogether."

Her tired mind wandered immediately and she tried to pull it back from her grocery list to God.

"I wish I was better, God. I'm sick of my life. I'm sick of my husband being gone. I'm sick of scrubbing pen marks off walls. I'm sick of kid's songs and I need more sleep."

She felt better. At least it was out in the open.

She pictured John standing in the sink, naked except for the fire man's hat, spraying the hose across the room at the lit burner. Angela started to laugh. There were other people in the church so she put her head in her arms and tried to control herself. Her father was right. The temptation was too much for him. She would let her father tie off the hose.

Angela prayed the Allegiance Prayer and then sat back in the silence, contemplating the Crucifix. She had decided to quit work and remain home with these kids. It was her decision. With Dan working the hours he had to work, there was no way she could leave even part-time because for this period in their lives, Dan couldn't help out much at home. It was fair that the children get what they needed and Angela wanted them to get it from her. There were just some days that it was really hard and recently the days had begun to drag. She would look at the clock, hoping for noon and it would not even be eleven. More children's shows, more juice, more messes.

"Help me, Jesus," she prayed. "Help me to be cheerful. It's not their fault I'm tired."

She thought of her two babies. They were so funny. They loved each other, when they weren't fighting, and they loved their parents. There was a lot of love in the house, she knew, despite Dan's long hours and their mutual fatigue. She had to work constantly through the feeling that it was all unfair in that Dan never got up during the night. Dan seldom stripped the sheets or scrubbed the walls. Dan got to leave every day. Dan's life seemed easy compared to hers.

He might not see it that way, she knew.

"It seems unfair, Lord," she prayed. Staring at the cross, she felt a moment of grace. Jesus, hanging there, knew something about injustice, she realized.

"It was unfair to You, too, Lord," she acknowledged, studying His figure. "I love my family, Jesus. Help me to be better. Help me to be happier scrubbing walls and cleaning up messes."

She thought of something her mother told her. Her mother said that it seemed unfair when the children were little but that as they grew, things became more equitable. That was something to look forward to and if she could hold on to that maybe she could stay away from the bitterness that tempted her to be unhappy. It seemed like a lot of people had it easier than she did but then she considered that there were plenty of people who had it worse.

Angela thought of a young mother battling leukemia and she rose immediately to light a candle for the sick woman. That would be worse. And Dan was good, she mused. Generally, if he was not working, he was home, except for basketball and did she really want him to quit basketball? No.

"What makes me happy, Jesus?" she asked. "Clean walls? What do I want to do that fits in with these babies?"

She considered this moment. If she could have a small bit of time alone each day, or even every other day, perhaps she could keep her life of service in perspective. She needed time to pray. She needed to get to Mass whenever possible. Her father had been right to send her here and she prayed for him with gratitude. She thought of a neighbor and thought maybe they could take turns watching each other's children twice a week. If she asked her parents for one hour a week, that would be three days. She usually saved her parents for doctor and hair appointments but this was important, too.

The other thing she had to do was get the kids outside. They all needed exercise. They went stir crazy in the house.

Angela sat planning. She needed a few adjustments and a tighter schedule and the situation would improve.

Dan popped into her head and she thought about her marriage. The right thing to do was be supportive and cheerful. She cringed, thinking of how unappreciative he seemed. He had no idea of how hard she worked to keep the house liveable. Could she live with that?

That was difficult. She resolved to talk to him and try to let him know how she was feeling, praying it would not end in a fight. She tried to put herself in his shoes. She would stop complaining about his basketball. He needed to get out. Fine. So did she. Maybe Angela would take Saturday afternoons. If he had to work, Angela would hire a babysitter. She would not argue or get angry. She would just do it.

When Angela walked out of the church, she had a plan. She felt better than she had in weeks.

An hour later she carried groceries in the front door.

The first thing she saw was the diaper rash smeared wall. As Grandpa had said, it wasn't too bad. The second thing she saw was that the couch had been moved to block access out of the living room. Her father sat on the couch reading a book to Martina. John, wearing his Fire Chief hat, held a three-foot piece of rubber tubing.

"Hi, Mom," he shouted. "I have a real fire hose."

"Great," Angela answered. "Where did you get it?"

Her father turned around. "I had it in the trunk. The TV is the fire. It's turned to a nothing station. We turned the sound down and adjusted the color all the way to the right. It's reddish. He has to put that fire out every time the bell rings. Watch."

Her father indicated an upside down bowl with a spoon next to it on the coffee table. He picked up the spoon and banged it against the bowl.

"Ding, ding, ding," he shouted. John ran for his boots and winter coat. "That's his gear." Suitably dressed, John stepped into a cardboard box from which the bottom had been removed. He picked up the box and his hose and ran three times around the living room making siren noises while Martina clapped her hands. Finally, he stopped in front of the TV, stepped out of the 'truck,' and began to put out the fire, making water noises. Angela, still holding her groceries, cheered with Grandpa and Martina.

"Well done, John. Good work," her father applauded. "You saved the building. What about the Barbies?"

"I forgot the Barbies," John shrieked. He grabbed two Barbie dolls from on top of the TV and threw them into the cardboard box. "That's the ambulance, Mom. They have to go to the hospital. That's Martina's job."

"Wow," Angela said. "This is some game. Why is the couch moved, Dad?"

Her father smiled. "I outsmarted them. As usual, they split up on me. I followed John into the bedroom and while I was in there helping him collect his gear, Martina put three potatoes in the toilet. I saw her heading down the hallway with the potato masher so I gave chase. She was trying to mash them when I caught her. Uh…they're still in there. I had to contain the kids and establish a perimeter so I moved the couch." He smiled at his daughter. "Nobody's hurt. Nothing is broken. And there are no additional messes, if you don't count a few spuds in the toilet."

Angela laughed aloud as she carried her bags to the kitchen.

"Potatoes in the toilet are nothing around here. Thanks a million, Dad."

This day had certainly shaped up.

Morning in One of God's Families

Just before dropping off to sleep, fourteen-year-old Connor said the Allegiance Prayer. He was cutting his prayers very short but didn't care. It had been a terrible day. The next day promised to be even worse. "God, please help me tomorrow," he prayed.

Across the room, his little brother Jack thought guiltily about a lie he had told. "God, I'm sorry for the lie. I don't know what to do about it."

Down the hall, sixteen-year-old Roberta asked God to help her be nicer to her brothers.

Their mother prayed silently for all of the children.

Connor awakened from sleep to the sound of rummaging. He spotted his younger brother Jack taking a pencil out of his school bag.

"Get out of my bag," he roared, lunging from his bed.

Jack jumped in alarm and ran from the room.

Connor made his way to his school bag. He was in high school. He tried to keep his things straight but his brother and his brother's friends got into everything. It wasn't fair. Yesterday he got a detention for not having his paintbrushes for art. He knew his brother had taken them but he couldn't prove it. When challenged, Jack had denied the accusation but Connor knew he was lying. Connor considered putting a mouse trap in his backpack. That would be excellent revenge. For now, he had to go back to art without the brushes again because he had not been able to find them.

"Connor," shouted his mother from the kitchen. "Breakfast is ready."

He dressed quickly and headed into the day. Jack and Roberta sat at the table eating. His younger brother looked like the perfect child instead of the thief that he was.

"Mom," he said angrily. "You have to keep the Annoying Kid out of my stuff."

His mother flared at once. "Do not call him that. Jack has a name, Connor, and it is ugly the way you talk to him."

Jack stopped chewing long enough to smile at his brother angelically.

"Jack knows I need my stuff for school, Mom, and he steals everything. He broke my crocodile head yesterday. I just found it hidden under my bed. I'm going to kill him if he touches anything else."

"Connor," his mother said sternly, "stop threatening him. He's only eight. You were the same way when you were eight."

"I wasn't a retarded menace," Conor snapped.

Perfect Roberta looked up from her breakfast, "Yes you were," she said brightly. "I can vouch for the fact that you were a retarded menace when you were eight. And now you smell. Do you ever shower?"

Furious, Connor shoved the box of cereal across the table at her.

"That's enough," his mother retorted. "Everyone be quiet and eat your breakfast."

Connor sat sullenly, considering injustice.

Jack got away with everything. His sister was a superior witch. Nothing seemed fair in this house or indeed, anywhere. Did he really smell? Connor finished his breakfast and headed back to his room, looking for the bag of paintbrushes.

"Connor," he heard his mother call from the kitchen. "Hurry. We'll be late."

He did not answer but got down on his knees and began pulling things from under his bed. This was where he had stuffed all of his clothes yesterday when his mother made him clean his room. He found a can of deodorant and sprayed his sweater. He had showered yesterday so he figured it must be his school sweater that smelled. The fumes made him cough and he put the can back under his bed, considering that perhaps he had overdone it. Where had the bag of paintbrushes gone?

The door to his bedroom swung open and his mother towered over him with a look of frustration on her face. "What in the name of heaven are you doing? We're late."

Connor's voice rose in spite of himself. "I'm looking for my paintbrushes. The Annoying Kid stole them and I got a detention yesterday for not being prepared. I can't go without them."

His mother sighed deeply. "Why do you tell me these things in the morning when we're already late? What can I do about it now? We have to go or we'll all be late."

Connor felt ugly inside and fought the urge to cry. "I'm not going back there without them. She embarrassed me in front of the whole class. I'll get another detention. She said, 'Connor, how hard is this?' and everyone started laughing."

Connor felt his color rising as he thought back on it. "I hate Jack. He takes everything."

"You don't know that Jack took them," his mother replied. "You're assuming he did and I agree that he probably did but Connor, sometimes you lose things. You're disorganized. It's not always Jack's fault."

Connor continued to pull things from under his bed as his mother put down her purse and began to help him, looking under Jack's bed.

"Mom," he said, still fighting tears, "you let him get away with everything. I wouldn't be disorganized if I didn't have to share a room. Roberta gets her own room. And did you hear what Roberta said? She said I smelled. She is constantly mean to me and you don't say anything to her. I hate her, too."

"Roberta was mean and I told her that when you left the room. You don't smell. Roberta is just very sensitive to smells for some reason."

"I hate her and I hate Jack, too. And I hate my art teacher and I hate school. Gerry McIntyre slammed me into a locker yesterday in front of everyone."

His mother sat back on her heels. "Connor, that's terrible. Why didn't you tell me?"

Connor felt his eyes fill up in spite of himself. "What's to tell? I got the detention for language because I called him a name. Naturally, the teacher didn't see him push me. She got there just in time to hear what I said to him."

"Did you tell her?"

Connor started to cry in earnest now, hating himself for it. "No. If I told her he'd get a detention and then he'd come after me even more. So I got two detentions yesterday and neither one was my fault. Nothing is fair."

"MOM," screamed Roberta from the front door, "I'm going to be late. Let him walk if he's not ready."

His mother ignored her. "I'm going to write a note about the brushes, Connor. Your teacher will understand if I tell her that Jack took them. He said something about painting mud pictures yesterday. What are we going to do about Gerry McIntyre? I should talk to someone at the school."

Connor gave her a look of horror. "Are you kidding? I'll die if you do. I'll never tell you another thing."

He fought back tears as the door flew open. Roberta, immaculately dressed and perfectly organized, stood, great and terrible, staring down at them.

Suddenly, her face contorted and she began to wave her arms. "What is that smell? Is it aftershave?"

"Roberta, please," her mother said quietly.

Roberta looked at her brother and noted his face and her

mother's countenance.

"What's up?" she asked.

Her mother replied. "Connor is missing paintbrushes and he got two detentions yesterday. Neither one was his fault but the teachers did not know that because he didn't tell them. Roberta, do you know Gerry McIntyre?"

"Mom," groaned Connor. "Don't tell her."

"Don't tell me what?" Roberta demanded. "What's wrong, Connor? Gerry McIntyre is an orangutan. He's always in trouble. Tell me what's wrong."

"Mom," shrieked Jack from the front door. "I'm out here in the car by myself. Is anybody going to school?"

"Let me get him inside," their mother said, rising from the floor. "We'll all just have to be late."

Roberta dropped her backpack to the floor. "The world won't stop if we're late, Mom," she stated. "You can write notes for us. Connor, tell me what happened. Right now."

Connor, badgered by his sister, spilled out his tale of distress. Roberta listened carefully, her own color rising in anger.

"The problem is lunch time," Roberta noted flatly. "It's always lunch time when he starts in on people. Go to the rec room instead of the cafeteria. I'll stay in the rec room with my friends in case he follows you. Connor, I know it's embarrassing but everyone knows it's him. It's not you."

Together, the brother and sister created a strategy so that Connor could avoid any contact with Gerry for the next few days.

"He'll start in on someone else," Roberta observed. She spoke thoughtfully. "If he doesn't leave you alone, we'll have to tell someone. I'll go with you if that happens. For now, though, keep walking away from him. Okay?"

Connor's eyes had long since dried. He felt better after

telling Roberta. Roberta was sensible. She understood why he could not let his mother go to school.

"Okay," he agreed.

The door opened the smallest bit. Roberta and Connor watched silently as a muddy bag of paintbrushes flew into the room. Jack's footsteps pounded away down the hall. They burst out laughing.

"The missing paintbrushes," Roberta said. "Mom must have guilted him into a confession. Wash your face. I'll scrub the paintbrushes."

Connor rose, consoled and comforted.

It never occurred to them that God had answered everyone's prayers.

The Commute

Traffic slowed to a creeping pace and Luke released a sigh of frustration. He found himself perpetually frustrated these days. If it wasn't work, it was his relationship with his girlfriend. And there never seemed to be enough money to do what he wanted to do. Nothing seemed to be going well.

He glanced down at his dashboard. Seeing the bright Holy Card fastened there, Luke recited the Allegiance Prayer.

"I give You my life, work and heart, God," he said to himself. "Good luck with it. My life is full of uncertainty, my work is unsuccessful, and my heart is filled with pain."

He sighed deeply again as he started, stopped, started, stopped, lurching along the highway with thousands of others. Luke kept the radio off for half of his drive each morning. It was a small offering he made to heaven in exchange for a prayer answered. Luke believed that God heard his prayers and he also believed that it was just and fair that he thank God when God answered his prayers. He had a landmark halfway to work and when he passed it, he switched on the radio each morning.

He sighed again, bored and edgy.

Glancing around to other drivers, Luke noticed a woman in the next lane. She drove a new BMW and looked like she lost little sleep worrying about money. Additionally, Luke noted that whatever she did for a living, she could quit and do fashion modeling at any time. She was beautiful.

Must be nice to have it all, he thought bitterly.

Luke caught himself. This bitterness was a problem. What did he care if some woman had looks and money? Being alone with himself and his thoughts was harder than being at work sometimes. "Take away this anger, Jesus," he prayed, trying not to be frustrated by his lack of peace.

Traffic stopped dead and Luke studied the woman even more closely. Suddenly, an intuitive light came to him.

"She's miserable," he said to himself in wonder. He did not know how he knew this but he knew it as much as he knew his name and age. "She feels like nobody loves her."

This knowledge was so clear, so profound, and Luke was so blasted with the truth of it that he felt a little shaken. Marveling, he tried not to stare. For the briefest moment, he glimpsed the woman as Jesus glimpsed her. So overwhelming was Luke's compassion, his pity, that he instinctively began to pray for her.

"God, help her to see that You love her," he began earnestly. "Help her to see that she is pleasing to You and that You have a plan for her and that her heart is safe with You. Help her not to be troubled by the cruelty of those around her. Let her rise above the circle of companions, Jesus, so that she can see her life with Your truth. Give her peace and calm, Jesus. Please, Jesus. Give her dignity back to her, Lord."

Honking horns snapped Luke from his place of petitioning and he resumed the lurching pace. The tears in his eyes startled him. Where had that come from? Luke could not remember praying like that since his mother's death. And the knowledge of her pain? He had felt like he could see it, it was so transparent to him. Rather than disliking her for her obvious financial comfort and beauty, he experienced her anguish in a tidal wave of emotion that left him limp.

"God help her. Please," he concluded. "Help me not to be so angry that I ignore the pain of the people around me."

All previous irritation lifted. Luke drove on, thinking about God's compassion for humanity. He wondered how God managed to stand the pain of loving people this much.

The landmark for switching on the radio came and went.

Today, Luke completed the drive in silence.

Part Four

The Mountain View

December 16, 2006

Today I saw a vision.

I was brought to the mountain of holiness. I am at home here on this mountain in that I have seen it on many occasions. I saw the mountain as it looked approximately one hundred years ago. There were a great many people on the mountain at that time, climbing steadily and there was a general upward motion in that so many climbed that it propelled everyone up. If a person looked around, he would see most of his friends and family climbing with him and he would be less likely to be distracted by the world and drawn down into it, away from the path to God.

Jesus then informed me that He wanted to show me the condition of the world today. I saw the same mountain. Here and there a few stragglers climbed but they were isolated and the presence of God's children on the mountain was sparse. Compared to the vision of times past, the difference was startling. The ones climbing at this time were laboring hard and were being constantly assaulted from behind, from souls not on the mountain but in the world. These assaults included scorn, ridicule and slander. They climbed despite these attacks and kept their eyes on heaven with great determination and deliberation.

They keep their eyes on God through something we can call a heavenly gaze. I understand this gaze so clearly. It is the Holy Spirit which unites Christ in each one of us to the Father in heaven. The gaze that moves from Christ in each soul to the Father is so strong in these souls climbing the mountain that they do not turn away. They are protected by the power of this gaze which holds them safely in the divine will.

Even amongst holy ones, though, there is the noise of the world tempting them. Some holy souls drift toward the outer limits of this gaze and risk turning toward the world. Pride is the greatest danger amongst holy souls. Obedience protects against pride.

I am at such a loss. I do not want to try to describe this as I am afraid of falling so far short. I am having the greatest difficulty. Dear Father, sustain me. I am acutely aware of the momentousness of this.

I saw a line of demarcation at the bottom of the mountain. I will call this the Ring of Defiance. People there faced the world, but from the base of the mountain. They claim holiness based on their position at the foot of the mountain. They use their position to allow themselves to be viewed as superior to both those behind them, true holy ones climbing, and those before them, souls in the darkness of the world. They jeer at people who approach God's mountain from the world, turning souls away from the process of approaching God. I understand that these ones have created a barrier to God's children. They include hypocrites, disobedient priests, those who are greedy for material things, and others in religious life who use their position for personal gains, such as ego or financial gains, power or what have you. I saw that misbehaving priests are a big problem in some areas at this time. I know many holy and beautiful priests and this causes me the greatest pain to write this but I am trying to accurately represent what I saw. Hypocritical lay people are also a terrible problem, it is true, and I saw many lay people in this line. These people may have had good intentions but they stopped climbing, a process which requires effort and self-sacrifice.

This line of souls is being used by Satan to block access to God. There is a terribly sinister mood among this group and they relentlessly ridicule holy souls. This is unpleasant in the extreme.

Please understand that this vision represents my understanding of the state of the world at this time.

I had the greatest sense of an emergency situation here. There was terrific activity in the air around the mountain. I saw angels taking souls from the world and carrying them to different levels on the mountain. This is an opportunity that some are being given at this time because of the nature of the emergency we are facing. Some take to this abrupt increase in holiness and rejoice at God's goodness. Others remain on the mountain for a time but then descend to a level that requires less sacrifice. This is painful for Jesus in the extreme as His great gift that is a huge outpouring of grace is being rejected. Jesus is bringing many souls to high levels with little effort on their part. If one could see the light from the souls climbing in times past, one would have a hope of understanding the dearth of light at this time. You see, there are far fewer souls on this mountain now allowing God's light to flow through them. This is why the world is in such darkness. At the same time, I see that God is sending light in a generous way through those on the mountain. The higher souls are on the mountain, the greater the blast of light that flows through them. There are many obscure souls who are sending terrific amounts of light into the world and who are completely unaware of how God is counting on their holiness as one of His assets during this time of emergency.

There is much more but I cannot really get words around it. I will try to put bare words on a glorious and bountiful experience. It is like saying wet to describe the ocean. It is so short of the truth that I hesitate to attempt.

God is using this mission and many like it to cry out to souls in the darkness of the world. I had a sense of our little booklets being handed to people in the darkness. I saw people read the booklets and then look up to God. God rushed to them, secured their willingness and an angel literally lifted them out of the world onto the mountain of holiness. The key about this fact is this. They are being lifted right over the heads of those who ring the mountain, attempting to block access. The angels are actually carrying people past these enemies. This is truly a rescue mission and God has given me a vision that allows me to understand what is happening. I wish I were an artist as I would draw it, so clearly do I see it.

I see that something is coming. It is great and terrible and I felt a sense of dread. Its power is fearsome. I asked God what this was because I knew well that it was not limited to one event. He answered, ***"Change."***

The change is going to be dramatic.

I saw little, smaller waves of change that came in advance and I understood them to be events like the tsunami, earthquakes, hurricanes and typhoons as well as man-generated difficulties. These are warning waves. I pray that God will compensate for any way that I may have failed to communicate this experience.

December 17, 2006

Today I found myself back at the mountain of holiness. I saw many people ascending at quite a high level. These ones made steady progress and seemed to exhibit great joy. I found myself among them for a moment in that I had the experience of how they felt. The mountain at this height was steep and there would be a risk of falling back but I sensed the most secure support at my back. It was like a solid structure against which to rest and it felt perfectly safe and absolutely sound. I saw, in looking around, that something bound us all together at this level and everyone around me was as secure as I was, which is what contributed powerfully to our freedom and subsequent joy. I said, "Jesus, what binds us together?" Jesus said, **"It is obedience to My Church, Anne. The solid support behind you is your obedience to My Church."**

I rejoiced in the happiness of those around me and delighted in the steadiness with which they moved, never backsliding. I understood clearly that if a soul left obedience the support would be jeopardized.

I asked Jesus a question because I am bothered by something. I said, "Lord, what about the cases where people act in obedience but are really unkind? They are obeying but something is terribly wrong."

Jesus drew my attention to the Ring of Defiance, the ring of people at the base of the mountain that repulsed others. I understood that while some appeared to obey in deed or in behavior, they lacked the spirit of obedience. Jesus told me that I would know quite quickly if the spirit of obedience was lacking in a soul because I would experience arrogance from these people. They pretend to obey but in their hearts they have no love. Their obedience feeds their arrogance and they use the pretense of obedience to hold themselves above others. People experience superiority and coldness from them. I know some of these people and it is very repugnant. They can be cruel and indifferent. It is another case of others being the mirror in which they admire themselves. I said, "Lord, they do a lot of work." He said *"Yes, and they demand full payment from Me. They present each deed to Me with a demand for recompense."*

I remained quiet, such was the dreadfulness of this. Jesus, in response to my unasked question said, *"They will be repaid for their deeds but they will spend time in purgatory learning about love and humility."*

I was very aware that those climbing the mountain could rest in their obedience when they became tired or discouraged. They could actually lean back into it for a time until their courage returned. God is pleased with this.

December 26, 2006

Jesus told me that He was going to show me more about the state of the world today and He brought me to the mountain of holiness. He drew my attention to the area on the outside of the Ring of Defiance. In the world, outside of the safety of the family of God, are many who are living in rebellion to the Church. We can think of them as fallen-aways. Jesus showed me two specific groups distinguishable from each other in this way. One group is made up of those who harbor a grudge against the Church, real, and constantly enflamed by the enemy. They have been hurt by someone claiming to represent Christ and His Church or by someone who claims to be an apostle of Jesus. They have been hurt by someone more or less acting as though they were acting in His name.

The other group is made up of those who are simply using this time of suffering for the Church as an excuse for disobedience. They have not been hurt by the Church or by anyone claiming to be holy. They are simply citing the grievances of others as an excuse for license. They will usually go the popular way or the easy way and I saw them as possessing weak character. For whatever reasons, they are not serving. I asked Jesus which group, of the two, was going to be more difficult to convert. He said the second group as they are not attracted to holiness because it entails sacrifice. He told me that the group who had been wounded and who walked in pain, bearing grudges, would have to be converted first and then they would draw the others back. The ones in the second group are followers, not leaders.

I asked the Lord to clarify and He gave me examples of three people. The first one is someone I know who does not act very holy. Jesus said she is safe because she is living within the confines of the family of God. *"She lives mostly for*

*the world and for material things but I can access
her. I am not blocked out because she attends
Mass and considers a relationship with Me de-
sirous. She intends to come to Me more completely
later, as many do. She is safe."*

The second woman is one who lived in the world in absolute rebellion to the Church. If asked why she did not attend Mass she would say that many priests had behaved badly
and this affected her faith in the Church. If asked a question
about Catholic doctrine, really the barest truth, she would appear perplexed, as though this were not something she had
been taught. This woman has used the pain of others as an
excuse to behave in a way that is not Christian. She is openly
defiant. She is not safe.

The third person is a man who had been hurt by a repre-
sentative of the Church. His wife was dying of cancer. Their
marriage was civil in nature as she had been married before
in the Church and had never sought an annulment. The
priest, correctly, refused to marry them in the Church. He
could not do so. Jesus said, *"This man has been hurt by
someone who acted in My authority but without
My compassion. If this priest had been united to
Me, acting in humility, he would have acted with
such love that this man would not have been
driven away by the truth of his situation. Clearly
this man will be accountable for his rebellion, as
this priest will be accountable for failing to love,
but I understand his wound and I see that this
man acts in love to those around him. I am in
pain for this man, Anne. I want him back in My
family and I want him back in My heart. He rejects Me so bitterly. I will heal him but he has
lived a great deal of his life without benefit of My*

love. Also, Anne, his bitterness influences others to bitterness as his complaint is valid."

I want to say something about this priest, lest anyone be confused. He did not injure this man by speaking the truth, but by his terrible indifference to the sufferings of the man's wife and the situation of her first marriage. The priest had no interest in helping this man, who came to him in search of Jesus for his dying wife. As such, an opportunity for both of these people to return to Jesus was missed.

I asked the Lord how we will convert the people who have been injured. He said, *"Many will be brought back by the love of lay apostles and by the writings given to the world in this mission. It is important, though, to understand the distinction between the two groups."*

I asked Him why this was important.

He said that the second group of people, who have no real grudge, no cause, will be more difficult to deal with and lay apostles must understand and accept this. It is the difference between someone who is actually ill and someone who pretends to be ill. I guess those in the medical profession will treat someone who is actually ill differently than someone who is pretending to be ill in order to avoid work or get attention.

Jesus says He is not referring to these people who have actually been hurt but to people who have not suffered, who are not injured, but who simply want to live without any accountability to heaven.

December 27, 2006

Today the Lord brought me back to the mountain of holiness. I saw a large group of people inside of the Ring of Defiance. They were safe, on the right side of the mountain in terms of being inside the ring, but they did not climb. This was hurtful to Jesus because He continually called out to them. They say, in summary, "Yes, Jesus, we know You are there. We know we are called but we do not want to come right now. We'll come later." Poor Jesus needs them to come now. The problem for them is that they are facing the world and they are distracted by the activity in the world. They know right from wrong, of course, and they do not live terribly sinful lives, but neither do they advance in holiness as they should. Some would call these people nominal Catholics.

They identify themselves as Catholics. They do love God and they reject the enemy but I would call them underachievers in the school of holiness. Their capabilities are not being expanded or developed and their performance for heaven is lackluster. Jesus loves them. There is no question, but He needs them to do better in order to assume their role in the renewal.

Jesus drew me out, back into the crowd of fallen-aways on the outside of the Ring of Defiance. I understood even more clearly that the ones in the second group who are taking advantage of the Passion time of the Church are not very nice company. They are further out from the mountain than the ones who have been wounded.

Beyond their location exists a group that works actively against Jesus Christ. This group is made up of souls who collude with God's enemy. Their goal is always to draw others away from Christ. They are sinister in their fixation on taking souls from God. They are evil. The frightening thing about being amongst this group, as I mystically experienced it, is that they are not what they seem from the eyes of the world. Some purport to serve humanity. Do they know they serve Satan? I would have to say with my limited knowledge that they know their enemy is the family of God. They hold themselves above holy ones. They are superior in their rebellion. They seek the destruction of God's plan and even though they talk of the good of humanity, if you pull on the strings of their theory and practice, you will find that there is always damage to humanity at the end of the line. I fear I am not being clear enough.

Just as an abusive person tells you that he is acting in your best interest, these people state that they serve the good of humanity. In reality, they do not. They serve their own purposes and the purposes of God's enemy.

To explore this further, the problem for the fallen-aways is that they are weak in virtue and they are vulnerable to be drawn into this group. You see, it is easy for them to step even further because it suits their selfishness. They can sin with greater and greater abandon in this group because all is not what it seems. Is it possible for someone to be in this group working against the family of God and be ignorant of what they are doing and therefore not accountable for their actions? That story will be told in their soul, of course, which is transparent to Jesus Christ and which will be equally transparent to the individual in the moment of his death.

If I were looking to determine whether or not a person existed in this far out group, I would look to see if their actions matched their words. Are their private behaviors consistent with their public positions? I would also look to see if the plans they promoted resulted in unity and peace in the hearts of individuals or discord in the hearts of individuals. I would also be looking to see whether the words they preached yesterday match the words they preach today. In other words, do their positions tend to shift with the breezes in the world? I would look for arrogance and false humility, along with an attitude of servility that is actually sneering. This can be concealed but there will be glimpses if one is looking.

The reason I write these things is because I saw political figures and leaders in this far out group. I think the point of this vision is to introduce us to the fact that there are categories of people in the world. The pull of the enemy gets stronger the closer one gets to this group of evil ones. Conversely, the pull to Christ gets stronger the closer one gets to the mountain. There is movement between the categories, of course, and this movement is, as I said, the cause of our hope and joy.

December 28, 2006

Today the Lord showed me the base of the mountain and I saw the Ring of Defiance. I saw again that just inside this ring of defiance is another ring, made up of people just barely on the mountain and not climbing, in other words, the nominals or underachievers. Jesus said, *"Look."* I did and saw that some were breaking away from the ring of defiance and beginning to climb because they heard the cry of Jesus. This was lovely to see and gave the Lord great joy. Jesus said, *"Look, Anne. These are lay apostles."*

The significant thing about this vision was as follows. When these people broke away from the others in the ring of defiance and the distance between the two groups grew, I could discern their differences more easily. Prior to that, it was difficult to distinguish between those who purport to serve the Lord but really serve themselves, the Ring of Defiance, and those who are good followers of Jesus but underachievers. This is a problem for many reasons.

The first reason is that the underachievers just inside the ring are not advancing in holiness as they should be. This limits both their personal growth and also the influence that heaven can have through them. They suffer and the family of God suffers. We have less personal holiness and a gap in service to the kingdom.

The second reason this is bad is because when others look from the outside of the ring, and I am referring to the fallen-aways at this time, they cannot get a good fix on appropriate examples of holiness. What is supposed to be a Christian is not very impressive if one is looking at those forming the ring of defiance. Those in the Ring of Defiance do not stand out but rather fit in with the world and as such do not draw others up the mountain. As I saw souls beginning to break away and advance up the mountain, I saw others being drawn to do the same. Those in the world can glance over at the mountain and see what real holiness looks like. They are being given more examples of true and authentic holiness, which attracts them. In this way the true servants separate from the hypocrites and those on the outside have something to accept, true Christianity, and something to reject, false piety.

Jesus needs more people to break away and climb the mountain of holiness. He cries out to them.

Mankind rejects Jesus and invites God to leave the world, indeed, often demands that God leave the world to itself. Jesus explained that if He withdraws His protective hand for the smallest moment, dreadful things can occur which include terrible disunity, which is the fruit of sin and rejection of God. God will not allow the world to continue on the course it has taken. He cannot allow the world to continue and still be responsible as our Father and the Father of creation.

I thought of those who would be angry and blame God for changes. Jesus was not affected by that thought and I understood that Jesus was more concerned with those who would look to Him and be converted to holiness. There are always those who reject God. In the same way, there are good people who accept God. They serve God and that is it. But there are also those who are indifferent to God because they think they do not need Him and they are lulled into complacency by the noise and deceit in the world. These souls, a great many, will only look to God when they see that they lack security. God is always there and God will draw them to Himself.

I cannot communicate what I have seen in terms of the feelings of the Lord. Let me say, simply, that Jesus is always right and Jesus is doing the right thing for us. It is the sins of mankind that cause our distress.

December 29, 2006

Today I saw the mountain again, and again noted the group who began to separate from the Ring of Defiance. The Lord showed me a terrific surge of people, like a charge, turning to Him and advancing in holiness. This is the renewal and this is how it will look, speaking mystically. There was a great increase in people on the mountain of holiness and it reminded me of before this time, in times past, when there was a greater number. The difference between that time and the time to come shortly is this. In the times past, the people on the mountain moved steadily together up this mountain. There was predictability and peace to it all. I was aware that what I saw happening now and in the near future was more abrupt, again, like a charge. I saw people encouraging each other actively, really pulling each other to advance with persistent urging. It was good and holy and founded in God's love. Those acting in God's name will always be kind and gentle, of course, and this is what I saw, but I did see great persistence and evangelization from apostle to apostle. I also saw people on the mountain urging each other to greater heights. This pleased the Lord.

Jesus said that He wants His name spoken, constantly and reverently. He wants us citing Him as the reason for our peace, our calm, our commitment. Jesus wants us all to talk about Him more and more and let His name, in that way, move freely throughout the world. This alone will increase His presence and the knowledge of His presence. We must all say His name with great frequency and reverence.

The last thing Jesus wanted to show me today was this. When the group of nominal Catholics departed for greater heights, I saw the separation from the Ring of Defiance. Jesus said, *"Look, Anne, what do you see?"* Well, I saw that those from the ring who were formerly nestled inside the lack of commitment of the nominal Catholics were now vulnerable to exposure. It was easier to identify what they really were. In other words, they were exposed because the nominal Catholics had departed for greater heights. They were identifiable as false, as I said.

I saw this as a positive thing.

Undated

I see the mountain. I see Jesus at the top. Beyond Jesus is an area that leads to and connects with God the Father. This area of light and truth is what I think of as the place of the divine will. Once we climb the mountain and enter through the narrow gate, that is, the heart of Jesus, we embark into the place of divine will. We secure ourselves there in this stream through obedience and move freely back and forth between the Father and the Son. We can exit this place if we are disobedient. This is a place of safety, a kind of grace place for those who are struggling. Jesus is all merciful and protective and seeks always to prevent us from leaving but if one wants to leave this place, one is free to do so.

I would say that people in this place are serving well, working for the family in the world.

I see that some souls enter into this place through hard spiritual work and self-denial. This is a place of humility. Great earthly honor and credit is not desirable when you are here. If a person chooses to exit this place, they drop down to the mountain below. They then have to renew the climb to the Lord and re-enter. Some do not, choosing instead to form the Ring of Defiance at the base of the mountain. This ring is made up of people on the mountain, barely, who face the world and repel others through their judgment and cruelty. They preach condemnation and routinely fail in love.

From this group, the Ring of Defiance, we also see those who are climbing a ladder up to the place of the divine will. This ladder is outside of the authentically climbing people, along one side of the mountain. They are the brigands and thieves. They seek to devour God's holy ones and will work steadily against God's chosen servants, claiming holiness that is a lie. In truth they work for the enemy of all of God's servants. The ladder extends up to and above the sheepfold. I want to be clear that only a liar and a thief would climb up this way. Those who climb this ladder understand what they are doing, attempting to gain access to the sheepfold for the purpose of evil. The greatest clues to their faulty motivation would be the presence of arrogance, along with a lack of charity. These are interested only in themselves, even while they cloak their love of self in love of God.

It is a long drop off this ladder and it cannot occur that one falls off the ladder and into the sheepfold. They fall the other way, where there is darkness. If they wish to repent, they fall to a safe place where they can begin an authentic climb. God loves each very much and we all desire that every soul join the family. We pray for these each time we pray for the conversion of sinners. It is ironic that these ones would never consider themselves sinners, preferring to be categorized instead as saints.

In the place of the divine will there is hard work and sacrifice but Jesus is there and the connection to the Father, our beautiful Father, is worth all of the sacrifice. When one observes the love He has for His children, one easily becomes committed to the cause of each member of our family and one is, through Him, also connected to the brothers and sisters who have gone before us. These, the saints, and also the ones who will be saints, surround us with protection and love, sending guidance and courage and all that is good and necessary to sustain us.

This is the way it works. It is this that the Lord wills for our experience on earth.

Part Five

In Defense of Obedience
and
Reflections
on the Priesthood

Spring 2007
Jesus

My beloved apostles seek to serve Me in each moment. This gives Me cause to rejoice. My heart lifts especially at any act of obedience made to the authority I have placed with the Church. I intend to unify all apostles serving in this time. If your heart is with Me, your Jesus, you will feel the urge to align yourself in humility to the decisions made by the authority of the Church. It is this that I ask of you. It is this that I require from you. My beloved ones, it is this that will increase the speed of the renewal. Rest often in My Eucharistic heart. There you will find the discernment you need to abandon any path of disobedience that is leading you away from My will. Perhaps this is not a concern for you because you are already respectful of My authority in the Church. This is good. But if change is necessary for you, you may be assured that I will not leave you without prompting and guidance. You seek liberation from any self-will that draws you from Me. I, also, seek this for you. Perhaps you feel that your life cannot be changed immediately but you are willing to embark on a process of change to adjust your course. Be at peace. It is I who prompts the course adjustment. I will see to it if you allow Me.

In Defense of Obedience

In this period of history, as in every period, there exist many realities which call for change. Human beings must always seek to perfect their behavior toward each other and this continuing process of improving man's condition is positive and necessary and, I believe, blessed and ordained by God. This stated, I believe that certain current attempts to improve mankind have spiralled into a widespread spirit of disobedience.

The concept of obedience is not a popular one during this time. More popular concepts include choice, freedom, and liberation. But do we really accept that people have the choice to hurt others and the freedom to sin without correction? And from whom do we wish to be liberated? From God?

How could good intentions have gone so badly wrong leaving us in this present sad condition? In response to those who object to the description of our condition on earth as sad, let me say that I am speaking from the standpoint of one who seeks to see with the eyes of Our Lord, Jesus Christ, who loves mankind and ordains peace and self-acceptance in all followers. I do not see peace in most people. I do not see in people an awareness of their bountiful dignity. It is my belief that a great many of God's children lack self-acceptance.

This is not a fruit of unity with God but of disunity, which I believe comes in part from a spirit of disobedience.

Why obey? How much should one obey? Should one obey sometimes? All the time? When one agrees with the given instruction? Should one obey when one disagrees? Should one go against one's better judgment in order to obey?

It is not the goal of this writing to make judgments on any individual. I will have to examine this concept in terms of my own experience and trust the Lord to shed light on it if He so wills.

There have been many times in my life when I was tempted to disobedience. First, there was a period of time when I lived away from the sacraments. I made rebellious decisions and kept non-Christian company. I suffered commensurately and it soon became clear to me that the world did not love me. I was mercifully drawn back to Jesus, through Mary, and He provided for me spiritually, mentally and emotionally.

Later, when I had returned to the Church, I struggled on another level. It was a process to align my life personally to the Lord's will and the teachings of the Church. I knew that I had to do so, however, and I embarked on the process.

During this time of personal struggle, I also experienced a temptation to systemic disobedience against the Church.

The Church gives clear teaching on birth control and contraception but science has advanced in such a way that we can generally prevent conception when we wish to do so. I worked in the women's movement and saw horrific exploitation and abuse of women and their children. It was difficult for me to reconcile myself to the Church's teaching at first. I understood that I was called to obey personally, but I was not convinced that this teaching was best for everyone. I lacked knowledge. Once I obtained the knowledge and understood the Lord's plan for women, I began to see that it was disobedience, not Church teaching, that threatened the well-being of women and children. The Church's teaching provides protection for the dignity of women and children and the Natural Family Planning Method is scientific and safe for women. God's way is the right way and I believe the Church is acting according to God's will in these matters.

If one openly disobeys a Church teaching, one is in essence saying that one wants the responsibility of leadership, which God has not given. One is, through disobedience, wresting authority. I believe that God puts Church leaders in positions of responsibility with the hope that they will obey the Church authority, helping them to grow in personal holiness and furthering unity in the Church.

We must accept that we may not understand everything about each directive we are called to follow. We may not have all of the facts. God treats some things on a 'need to know' basis.

One could observe that individuals will only disobey when they feel the Church authority in their life is getting it wrong. Most of the time, perhaps, they will obey. But where does this end? And if this is the case, then nobody is in charge, least of all God. I fear that those who cut and paste in the area of obedience to the Magisterium will find themselves in a position where their peace is destroyed and their effectiveness, from heaven's perspective, is diminished.

God can't count on them. They might obey, they might not. This disposition threatens His plan.

Decisions against the Church give Satan ammunition to use against us in our movement to personal holiness, which is our base mission here on earth regardless of who we are. The enemy uses this ammunition, our uncertainty and consequent vulnerability, to teach us about arrogance and to distract us from holiness. If we make a decision against the authority of the Church, we will have to spend a lot of time justifying it. We will possibly lie awake in bed at night arguing with nobody in order to prove to ourselves that we are right. We may come to know outrage, which fuels arrogance. Yes, we will exhaust ourselves trying to convince ourselves that we are right or, at the very least, justified in our disobedience.

Be alert. Satan will send people to support and encourage us in disobedience. We can always find someone who agrees with us. We must not seek the companionship of those who pull from unity with the Church. We must seek instead the counsel of those who encourage unity. These souls will have suffered. Their obedience will usually have cost them something and from these we will receive calm and wise counsel.

I understand that life is not black and white. I understand that many Church leaders cite compassion as a reason to disobey. They state, and possibly believe, that they are acting positively in response to the pain of their people. I understand this because I experienced the same thing in the women's movement. Despite this, I believe that the most compassionate assistance we can provide to others is the knowledge of God's truth and mercy in His teachings and the knowledge of God's continued presence in this world. Can we in good conscience deny truth to others in the name of mercy? Do we feel that God has denied others the capability and capacity for holiness?

Possibly at this time we disagree with a Church teaching or with the manner in which a Church teaching is being implemented. We are all thinking individuals after all and have the right to think in any way we like. We cannot stop our minds from consideration and it is often through consideration that we become reconciled and convicted.

Also, it is clear that each region and congregation experiences unique challenges and each individual will find his own struggle in his own mission field.

But I would say that Church leaders have a profound call to illustrate a spirit of obedience to the Magisterium for followers using the Church's teaching in the Catechism for guidance.

All must accept that there are times when we are not in charge, when we are called to follow, not lead, or if you will, to lead by following the authority.

Only if we remain small can God's bigness be seen. If we try to be big, we will obstruct the view others have of God.

At times, if we are to be obedient, we will have to make decisions against our personal will. We should expect this. As I said, we may even be called to make a decision to obey even though we may feel that the person in authority is mistaken. This is difficult indeed, perhaps the most difficult thing, but the fact that we are willing to do so illustrates humility, a trembling, a faith in a divine intellect that is greater than our own and a plan that is bigger than our own.

These decisions, the heroic acts of obedience, will put God in the absolute position of answering with His limitless power and I believe that the Lord is incapable of disappointing obedience.

As always, let us look to His example. Our Beloved One was "obedient even unto death" (Phil. 2:8). How palatable could the plan that was the Passion have seemed to the Eternal Victim? How sensible could it have appeared to His mother? Or His followers? Should Peter have persisted and cut down the soldiers who came to arrest Jesus? Should he have disobeyed, using his better judgment? Jesus said "No," and Peter stood down. The plan, the divine plan, unfolded in all its apparent senselessness.

God's plan was unfathomable to His apostles. This act of total sacrifice denied human rationale. Yes, on that day it is abundantly clear that God's plan mystified His followers.

We must accept that, like the early apostles, on any given day God's plan will mystify us. We are, after all, no better than our predecessors.

Our call to obedience is often a call to the heroic in terms of humility and faith.

To be clear, I am not advocating mindless servility. I am advocating fidelity to the decision we have all made to serve

Jesus Christ, according to His plan, in His Church.

Obedience is liberating in many ways.

First of all, it frees our mind. We do not have to wonder what to do in most given situations. If we cooperate with the authority in our life, Jesus can move us to holiness with great speed. If we do not cooperate, we do not allow Jesus to direct, and He will have to go slowly with us, in order to protect us. His goals will be jeopardized.

It is distressing to witness a spirit of pride and arrogance. We must always look for personal outrage as a marker for pride in ourselves. By this I do not refer to the outrage one feels regarding injustice done to others. This is appropriate. By this, the marker for pride, I refer to personal outrage associated with being treated less respectfully than we would like or being judged in a way that is less positive than we feel we deserve or desire. To clarify, we can go, as usual, to the Lord's example.

When people lied about Jesus personally or mistreated Him, He let it go, as in the Garden. He did not puff up and sputter in outrage. He was very consistent in behaving like a lamb.

But when people planned to stone an adulteress, He stopped them. He exhibited a sense of outrage, turning the situation on its head and using it to promote non-judgmental treatment of others.

Also, when He witnessed His Father's house being used as a market place, He exhibited outrage, even reacting with just anger.

Jesus quietly accepted personal insults and slights to Himself. He did not accept cruel behavior against people or blasphemous behavior against His Father.

There are those who will say that to behave in obedience is to offer up our free will. This is true. This is what we are striving for, to offer up our free will to the Lord. It is only when we give up trying to be masters that we can become servants. We will not enter heaven with our hands on our hips, telling everyone else, least of all Christ, where they are getting it wrong.

The former Holy Father, Pope John Paul II, made a statement on the ordination of women. In summary he said, "No. It's not going to happen." He issued an Apostolic Letter called *Ordinatio Sacerdotalis* detailing his thoughts. One of the observations he made was that surely if Jesus wanted women to be priests, He would have made His mother a priest. He did not. Jesus protected the separate and distinct roles of men and women in the Church. Nearly two thousand years later, the Holy Father Pope John Paul II protected the Lord's will by steering the Church in the direction God desired.

Some objected to the definitive nature of the Apostolic Letter. Then Cardinal Ratzinger made a statement that the matter should no longer be discussed. Waves of outrage erupted. How dare this man tell us what we can and cannot discuss?

This baffles me. Cardinal Ratzinger's statement seems to be an appropriate statement for a man of obedience attempting to support the correct and proper authority in his Church. I do not understand what others did not understand about this.

The fact that people wanted to continue discussing the matter after a definitive statement by the only appropriate authority is, in itself, evidence of a spirit of disobedience.

This is much like my children arguing over which movie we are going to see after I have stated definitively that we are not going to the cinema. The discussion is a waste of time and evidence that either their hearing is impaired or they are fighting for the sake of fighting.

Rather than be outraged, would it not have been better to think, in humility, Hmm. The Holy Father is serious about this. No doubt he has his reasons.

Would it not be wise to accept that God did not abandon the Holy Father with this important decision regarding the direction of His Church on earth?

Those of us who nourish similar outrage are wasting valuable time during which we are supposed to be working on our own movement to unity with Jesus and saving souls.

There are two paths. There is God's way, the path to personal holiness which is marked out by obedience and a spirit of humility. And there is the other way, Satan's path, which is marked out by pride and possibly grudging, bitter obedience, which leads to outright disobedience. Be aware that the spirit of personal outrage in us is always being stoked by the enemy in order to distract us from the job at hand, which is the divine will in each moment.

When we feel personal outrage we must run to Jesus immediately. This will prevent us from doing anything ridiculous or damaging.

With obedience comes humility and with humility comes obedience. You might say one feeds the other. Again, this does not mean we cannot question decisions or requests. It is normal to seek clarity when we do not understand. But we must do so respectfully, mindful of the presence of God in others and careful not to influence others to doubt. Those who challenge in arrogance know what I am saying and those whose spirit is false and duplicitous are known to God. How often the enemy speaks with pretend innocence and with no intention of accepting God's clarity. How often the enemy sets up a holy man for ambush. The enemy thinks he is very clever indeed but God reads souls, my friends. He knows what is in our hearts.

Now, if we are quite certain that a given human authority claiming to represent the Church has it wrong, clearly we have a dilemma and because we are dealing with humanity this can happen. In such times we must be very prayerful, saying, "Jesus, surely You are aware that You have a problem here." We must speak our conscience honestly, respectfully and privately to the authority in question and then leave the Lord to get on with His job, continuing on our walk to personal holiness via the path of obedience. Spiritual direction in these situations is invaluable.

To be sure, there will be times when we wonder if the Lord knows what He is doing. Doubts and fears will come. We may feel certain that the Lord's plan unfolding before us cannot possibly be successful. This is consistent with our humanity and consequent lack of divine vision. Our service in the face of these fears gives delight to God. But we must go along with God. If indeed our obedience and the decisions made by certain Church authorities result in disaster, it is the Lord's problem.

If we obey, if we decide for obedience and then walk hard and steady up that path, we will be free to become saints.

To retain a spirit of obedience, one must nourish an intimate relationship with Jesus Christ. It should be very personal to us, this relationship, because it is very personal to Him. All of our days should be spent in the awareness that we are in the presence of the Lord, who lays great stock in our acceptance of His will.

Jesus has plans and goals. He has designed in advance what He can do with our "yes" answer. His plan deals always with the salvation of our own soul, of course, but then Jesus works tirelessly for our loved ones and if we say "yes" to Him, He takes that "yes" and sees to our personal intentions first. This benevolence alone should melt us into willing servants.

There is Jesus Christ. We work to gain and retain unity with Him. This occurs through our willingness to do things His way. Then there is the Father, who radiates the divine will, perfect goodness. Between Jesus and the Father there is a stream, this divine will, an active, living, fluid exchange. The Holy Spirit is moving constantly between the two, connecting them. If we are united to Jesus through our willingness, He places us in this stream of light that connects us to the God-head. As far as we are willing to advance in holiness through our "yes" answers to God, Jesus advances us.

I believe that it is obedience that anchors us in this stream.

In this time, I see arrogance and superiority. I do not know about other times so I cannot speak of whether or not arrogance has increased or decreased or whether or not it is more prevalent or less prevalent than yesterday, but I can say that I see a lot of it now. The Lord has told me that this age is more disobedient than other ages and I believe Him.

To return to arrogance, there is a spirit of intellectual superiority that emits a steady flow of sarcasm. This is distasteful to Jesus. Better we limit our study to flowers in fields than contribute to this embarrassing and serious phenomenon that puts so many people off and limits the Holy Spirit. Many have educated themselves right out of reach of the Spirit. They say, in summary, "No thank you. I have no need for silent contemplation. You see, I have higher learning."

I am not objecting to higher learning and study. How could I when it opens the door to so many delightful possibilities? I am objecting to arrogance, superiority and spiritual suffocation. It is not Jesus Christ or the Holy Spirit encouraging people to believe they are superior to others. It is God's enemy. Those who read with humility will question themselves in this area. The Lord wants us to understand that even those with the highest learning on earth will find themselves pitifully unprepared for heaven if they do not contemplate daily how little they know. I have heard it said that only a truly wise man understands the depth of his ignorance. I believe this to be true.

To see a man with a lively intellect, with great learning, and with humility is surely a delight to the heart of our Savior.

Education, and everything else in our lives, should bring us closer to God and closer to obedience. If we find that we are moving away from obedience, noted by a feeling of superiority to those who obey, we must be alerted. We should embark on a course of Eucharistic Adoration, simply contemplating Jesus Christ in the Sacrament of the Altar. We must learn to love and we must learn from the Master.

If we do this, we will gradually begin to listen more and talk less. We will be less sure of our own opinions, open to the idea that we could be wrong about some things even while we are right about others. We will be more likely to accept the authority of those God has placed in our lives to lead us. We will come to allow others to fight the fight of words while we fight the fight of the spirit, the fight of holiness.

Dear friends, we must scrutinize ourselves. This is not an area where we want to get it wrong. If we generally believe we know more than others, we must turn toward the Lord and allow Him to educate or possibly re-educate our spirit.

A case in point is a wife and mother who recently told me that she was not very religious. She said that she had not read a great deal of religious books and therefore had little knowledge of things religious. I had, over time, opportunity to observe this woman with her children, her husband and in her life.

I said to her, "You may not be very religious, but you are extremely holy."

This baffled her.

I have met Church scholars who were very religious. They quoted learning from the early centuries and back, right up to the present. They knew lots of things that this wife and mother did not. I believe though, that if she were taken up to heaven right now, she would more or less fit in because she is all about service and love. She is all about sacrifice and humility. She is all about gentleness and respect for children and for the emotional protection of her husband, honoring the trust that he has placed in her through their marriage.

It has to be stated. This woman, according to heaven's goals which place personal sanctity first, is doing better.

Holiness is not a competition, of course. We only compete against our performance in the last five minutes, meaning we each need to try to do better than we have in the past. But look at what God must overcome in the wife and mother and then compare it to what God must overcome in the scholar.

Knowledge is not necessary for holiness. Humility is.

The wife does not think she is superior. She feels she must do better because she is not very religious. For the record, this woman never misses Sunday Mass and provides beautifully for the formation of her children. She lives in obedience to the Church. By religious she means saying the Rosary daily, reading religious works, and saying novenas and going on pilgrimages.

The scholar, on the other hand, is disdainful of this woman. He feels miles above her. He would not deign to speak to her for any length of time because he feels certain she is beneath him. If he would listen and observe, he would understand what this woman could teach him because she, through practice, has learned about prudence and generosity, kindness and forgiveness. She is actively practicing virtue and growing in holiness. She truly grasps religious concepts in her heart even though she lacks the words to describe them.

This, my friends, is the difference between running and talking about running. She is exerting herself. The scholar in this discussion is not.

I believe God is pleased with this woman and I believe God is hopeful that this scholar will learn humility.

Priests, in particular, must be wary of a spirit of superiority. Humility is very important to God's goals for their vocation.

To quote from the previously mentioned apostolic letter *Ordinatio Sacerdotalis* of Pope John Paul II to the Bishops of the Catholic Church on Reserving Priestly Ordination to Men Alone, *"Moreover, it is to the holiness and the faithful that the hierarchical structure of the Church is totally ordered. For this reason, the Declaration Inter Insigniores recalls: 'the only better gift, which can and must be desired, is love (cf.1 Cor 12 and 13).' The greatest in the Kingdom of Heaven are not the ministers but the saints (par. 3)."*

A first observation is that God wills that through their vocations, all priests become saints, but it must be underscored that the whole point of the priest's learning is to help God to raise up saints. This woman is part of the Body of Christ. She, and all individuals like her, are the point. One could say that her advancement in holiness is the goal for the priest's vocation and all that God puts into the priest's vocation should direct him that way. He is to minister to and thereby raise up saints, all the while admiring and standing in reverence of the grace present in those to whom he ministers. I pray for God's clarity in this point as it is so important for the humility of all priests.

With a trembling spirit I will say it this way. If a priest, of any level of authority in the Church, holds himself above those to whom he is called to minister, he needs to adjust his thinking.

We must not make a false god of education and learning or allow education and learning to persuade us that we ourselves are gods. We must use education and learning to examine our condition in relation to the example of Jesus Christ.

The authority with which a person speaks is the love and presence of Christ in his words. Knowledge is good, if it includes the presence and love of Jesus Christ.

Back to obedience, we can speak about obedience to God's Church and be technically correct but lack God's authority if we speak without God's love.

So perhaps there are two parts to obedience. There is obedience to the letter of the law and obedience to the spirit of the law. When one is missing, the other falters.

To take it further, if a Church leader acts in opposition to the authority of the Church, even given a stated intention of compassion and even assuming true compassion, he acts with only partial authority because he is acting without the letter of the law. If he acts in obedience to the Church and to the letter of the law but without the spirit of the law, which is God's love, he also lacks God's authority because he is acting in a manner inconsistent with the example of Jesus Christ.

One, love without obedience, or the other, obedience without love, produces incongruity that confuses the faithful and damages their trust in their priests, their Church, and by extension, their God.

Also, the Catholic Church must demonstrate unity and consistency for our brothers and sisters of other faiths who

watch us closely and to whom we owe, by heavenly obliga-
tion, a good example.

Clearly, the faithful in the Church rely on Church leaders
for direction. The Church does not point to itself, but rather
to Jesus Christ and to each individual's movement to unity
with Jesus Christ. Since eternity in heaven for the faithful con-
sists of and rests upon unity with Jesus Christ, then unity with
Jesus Christ must be the compelling goal for the faithful. The
Church, by heavenly design, encourages and promotes this
unity.

When a Church leader takes a public position against the
Magisterium, or even preaches in such a way that sows doubt
about the Magisterium, the message promoted is that the
Catholic Church, and by extension, Jesus Christ, is getting it
wrong. This seriously erodes confidence in the Church, and by
extension, Jesus Christ.

This doubt creates fear and anxiety in all the faithful, lay
and clergy alike, because it strikes deeply into the heart of our
trust in the Lord. Spiritually, many souls are distracted and
stumble. This creates an opening for the enemy to violently
shake the tree of our confidence in Christ and many fruits
that the Lord has taken years to cultivate can fall from our
souls to the ground, to rot and decay.

Disunity becomes apparent because some fall prey to confusion. Others, perhaps better rooted in obedience, will hold
the line. There will be conflict, though, a positioning of one
against another. We begin to resemble the enemy's legion,
bickering and undermining each other, tearing off in this direction or that one.

Also, the public disobedience of some leaves the clergy and
faithful who hold the line vulnerable. They may be marked as
cold, uncaring, out of touch, and lacking compassion. Their
authentic message of the Good News is weakened because

some, confused by the disobedience of others, distrust their motives and fail to correctly identify the truth.

Those who depart from obedience, even allowing for the motive of compassion, are stating, albeit maybe indirectly, that the Church, and again and always by extension, Jesus Christ, are not compassionate but they, the disobedient ones, are. They are standing with their back to Christ, drawing attention to themselves as the Savior, the Merciful One. They are drawing souls to themselves instead of directing souls to Jesus Christ. In doing so, they block the faithful's rightful view of God, who is the true source of all goodness and mercy.

To make an obvious observation, the humanity of each person insures that the presence of each person is temporary. Eventually all people depart, through relocation, retirement or death. If disobedient people have placed themselves as the draw, the goal for the faithful, their departure leaves a gaping hole where Jesus Christ, represented by the Church, should have been placed. I have seen this happen.

Clergy taking a public position of disobedience to the Church are encouraging the faithful to build their homes on unsteady ground. They are attaching their flock's spiritual security to themselves. Which man is steady enough, wise enough, and powerful enough to do such a thing? Only one Man existed who possessed these traits to perfection. He, Jesus Christ, has gone before us.

God wills that Catholics proceed always deeper into personal holiness through the path marked for them personally within the safe pasture of the Catholic Church. If the example set for Catholics by representatives of the Church is faulty and flawed, the faithful will be misdirected and misguided.

In this time, God wills that we move from an Age of Disobedience to an Age of Obedience. Think of this like a big boulder that must be shifted to another designated place. If we are to successfully shift this boulder and move it to the place God wills, we will need to act in unison. If part of the Body of Christ remains on the opposite side pushing against the faithful, the boulder will not move and we are exhausting ourselves, from the standpoint of the renewal, to no purpose.

Consequently, it is in our best interest, and clearly within God's will, that we assist our brothers and sisters in coming to the place of obedience, in both the letter and spirit of God's directions, made known to us through the authority of His Church.

Be warned. We must be compassionate in this effort and humble and merciful, but when dialoguing with those who are in error through disobedience, we must be certain that we stick to the intended goal which is to bring them to obedience, in both spirit and letter, and not the opposite, which would be allowing them to bring us to disobedience.

Silent contemplation of the Eucharist is, I believe, necessary for us so that we can hold God's line steady for Him and not be tempted to join the ones pushing against the boulder, that is, God's renewal.

As a caution, there exist subtle snares laid by the enemy. When one is confronted by genuine compassion in those acting against the Magisterium, one can be drawn into confusion. Many of these souls make excellent points in that there are areas in the Church which I believe the Lord wants improved. I see that the Lord is conducting change in these matters but through respectful dialogue, not rebellion. If I were curious to know what the Lord was concerned about in the Church, I would look at the Holy Father and see what areas are of concern to him.

Clearly, we must consider the return to obedience a process. Perhaps what is called for is a movement to obedience, a gentle shifting, directed by heaven, from one place to another.

God has willed a great renewal. It will happen. It is happening now.

We each have a role, willed by God, to play in this renewal.

This renewal will not advance through pride and disobedience. This renewal will advance through unity, which will be achieved through humility and obedience.

If you are rebelling against God's Church, I beg you, stand down.

"First of all, obedience is apostolic, in the sense that it recognizes, loves and serves the Church in her hierarchical structure" (P.73 *Pastores Dabo Vobis, Apostolic exhortation of His Holiness John Paul II on the formation of Priests*).

A Slice of Divinity

Jesus recently allowed me to learn about the priesthood through a series of mystical experiences. I will never view the priesthood or any priest in the same way.

I saw that at the moment of ordination, a slice of the divinity is placed into the heart of each priest. His soul is indelibly altered. This cannot be understood without examining the reality of the Trinity.

God, our Father, placed all of His goals and love for humanity into the heart of Jesus Christ, His Son. These things, the Father's goals and love for humanity, clearly cannot be removed from the heart of the Son.

At the moment of ordination, what I can only describe as a slice of the divine person of Jesus Christ, the First Priest, is stamped into the heart of the man. This cannot be removed, ever. I finally understood the statement that "once a priest, always a priest."

Within the soul of each priest is placed all of the love that the Father has for each person ever created. Within the soul of each priest is placed all of the hopes and goals that the Father has for each one of us. It is, quite simply, that big. These are the men that are called to be Fathers of God's children on earth.

This truth in no way diminishes another truth, which is that the laity are also called to possess Christ. The Dogmatic Constitution on the Church (Chap. 4) begins with a positive definition: the laity are those faithful who by virtue of Baptism are "made one body with Christ and are established among the People of God (L.G.31). No less than the clergy, they too share in the priestly, prophetic, and kingly functions of Christ; as such, they have a responsibility for "the mission of the whole Christian people with respect to the Church and the world." Yet it is emphasized that the laity carry out this responsibility in a manner entirely appropriate to them—they do so as non-office bearers. (The New Dictionary of Theology, p. 560.)

I once prayed for a priest who was dying. I felt sad for him because he was ill and his life was ending. Jesus said, ***"Anne, do not be sad for this man. The imprint of his vocation is already in heaven."***

Jesus then showed me what was occurring in heaven as this priest lay dying. People were gathering, joyfully exchanging their stories about this man who had corrected their courses, offered consolation at pivotal moments in their lives, or supplied them with great graces through the administration of the sacraments. I could see that this priest in his day-to-day service, which was humble, had little understanding of how much his work was impacting the people he served. Truly, heaven was altered because of this man's decision to serve us in the priesthood. I then rejoiced in the fact that this priest was nearly finished and that this wonderful celebration of his vocation and service awaited him.

I must report that the number of people awaiting him was in the thousands. The priest had no understanding that each life he touched through his vocation was connected to many other lives. The reward that Jesus prepares for those who serve Him is magnificent. In this time, the devil is trying to obscure the truth about the priesthood. I think of this like a House of Mirrors at a carnival. When we walk into such a place, we look at our reflection. In one mirror we might look ten feet tall. In another mirror we might look ten feet wide. Is it us in the mirror? Yes. Undeniably, it is us we are looking at. Is it an accurate reflection of us? No. It is a grossly distorted version of the truth.

In the same way, the devil has used the recent clergy abuse

scandals, among other things, to propagate a distorted vision of the priesthood. The reality is that a comparatively small number of priests served God's enemy by abusing others. They did not represent God but God's enemy when they did this. The pain they caused was and is shocking. We are all called to the ongoing ministry of the recovery of each victim, even if our ministry is limited to prayer for all victims and their families.

The enemy always seeks to tear down the Church. Each apostle is called to do the opposite, of course, which is to lift up the Church through our fidelity and obedience to the Magisterium.

I think of this period as a time when we are all stuck in a big puddle of mud. We've all been wounded, scandalized and sullied in some way by these scandals. This has been excruciating for our faithful priests, who are entitled to and deserve our constant love and support.

But now it is time to step out and move on. We are called to turn our backs to the past and look to Jesus Christ and to today's service and tomorrow's triumphs. I believe that Jesus Christ and all of heaven want us to move now, forward, onward, to great holiness and great renewal. I am certain that Jesus is sending a massive rush of grace to aid us all in recovering. It will happen. It is happening now.

I often think that without humility, we cannot have holiness. The enemy sends humiliation, it is true, but through these humiliations God brings humility. Since we must have humility for holiness, then humiliation, as painful as it is, can be partially viewed as a means to a wonderful end. Who cares how we get humility, as long as we have it?

The Church will survive this current attack as She has survived each past attack and as She will ultimately overcome each future attack.

Reflections On the Priesthood

A priest makes a decision to enter into the relationship of knowing God, of seeking Him. Through this decision, Jesus is able to possess the priest as an outpost, a dwelling place for the Godhead on earth.

With God's grace, I can see Christ in the priest on his ordination day and I can see Christ in the priest on the day of his death. I have also seen Christ in priests in heaven. They all look the same to me in that Christ is Christ on the ordination day, the day of death, and into and for eternity. So while the priest moves through his life in humanity, with doubts and imperfections, Jesus has no doubts and imperfections. Jesus serves humanity through the priest in His perfect divinity. I am as delighted by Christ in the priesthood as I am by Christ in the words He sends or Christ in the Eucharist or Christ in the heavenly experiences of Him that I have been allowed to have. It is for this reason, I believe, I feel such love for priests, regardless of their condition.

Given this, the Lord's mystical presence in the soul of the priest, it is clear that we must honor Christ's presence in every priest. It is easier to do so when a priest is willingly connected to that divine presence. It is more difficult, but more compelling I believe, to love the priests who are struggling.

Perhaps a priest is working against the kingdom. This is a dishonor to the covenant entered into by both God and the man at ordination. This is serious for the priest personally, of course, but also there is the gap in service and subsequent lag in the coming of God's kingdom that results. The priest's non-service affects many. We must target these priests for rescue through love, intercessory prayer, and honest appeal.

Each reader must accept that I am not talking about assaulting a priest for his choice of spirituality. There are those who so love the path they have been called to in the Church that they believe that unless others are following that same path, others are getting it wrong. A priest does not have to be "into" this or that apostolate to be holy. A priest has to be "into" the presence of Christ in his priesthood.

What I am saying is that while it is good to introduce the priests in our lives to the spiritual movements that are helping us, we should not make judgments about these priests based on their acceptance or non-acceptance of a particular spiritual movement.

There is something so beautiful about the priests that I have seen in heaven. One particular priest I saw represented was not actually there yet. He was coming soon, but I saw his imprint in heaven, the shape of him in that his presence was evident through all of the fruits of his labor. There were many in heaven waiting for his arrival, people whose lives he has impacted through his vocation.

While the priest serves on earth, Jesus prepares his eternity. This is the same for all of us but priests have something different that endures for eternity. They have the mark of Christ on them in a more concrete way. Heaven is different because of this man's vocation and the vocation of every serving priest. Heaven is altered. There is more glory for God because this man allowed Christ to flow through him in administering the sacraments and providing assistance to others with regard to direction, affirmation, and confirmation of what is God's will and what is not God's will.

It strikes me that the priesthood is under a ferocious attack. The sins of a few have been used by the enemy in an attempt to strip the dignity from many. Nobody can strip dignity from another, though, least of all from a man who shares the divine priesthood with Jesus Christ. I am keenly aware of the dignity of the men who are ordained priests. I am also aware of their sinfulness in the same way as they are aware of the sinfulness of others in that we are all asked to serve in our humanity, but I understand that their humanity can provide them with the humility to make them beautiful in God's eyes. How God loves them and rejoices in them.

I would encourage each priest to rejoice in his humanity, just as God does. And just as each priest should rejoice in his humanity, at the same time, each priest should rejoice in the divinity of Jesus Christ and in the divine nature of Christ present in his vocation.

Sinfulness, the propensity toward sin, is not a problem for Jesus. He can work through us in spite of our human nature which pulls us to selfishness. I see priests working and I see God's presence. They are connected, God and the man. They are united. The Father's eyes do not leave the priest because the Father's Son is within the soul of the priest and His goals, the Father's, rest in the heart of the Son. The Father's love for each child on earth is contained in the Son which is then transmitted into the heart of each priest. Truly, only in heaven will the priest see the scope of what God places in his soul at ordination.

Nobody can strip the dignity from a man such as this.

A priest should never worry about his humanity, as I said. He should fight always to resist temptation, of course, but he should understand that Christ will always be good and His goodness resides in the priest. When the priest falls, Christ remains standing. Christ will not stop being good simply because we stop being good. It is this that should comfort us when we are tempted toward discouragement because of our ongoing imperfection.

How does Jesus feel about His priests? How can we make a comparison in human terms that will do justice to the feelings of the Savior for these men?

Imagine first how the Father felt toward Jesus. Jesus was His Beloved One, of one and the same divinity, perfectly committed to the will and goals of the Father despite terrific hardship. At total personal cost, Jesus pursued the Father's goals.

The Father's goals often did not make sense to those who worked with Jesus. The world viewed Jesus as foolish at times. The world persecuted Christ. Christ persevered despite everything. Nothing the world threw at Christ diverted Him from the path the Father had chosen for Him.

Imagine how the Father viewed His Son.

The Father views each priest in the same way. They are part of Him as Jesus is part of Him. Each priest will rest with the Father in His heart. Not near His heart, but in His heart because truly when a priest pursues ordination, he is pursuing oneness with God.

Jesus Christ shares a brotherhood with each priest. He stands with the priest, in union with God and through the Holy Spirit. When the priest speaks for God, God sends the grace to accompany the words. The fact that the recipient of the priest's speech and counsel may not be open to the Holy Spirit present in his words in a given moment or in an immediate moment in no way diminishes the divine at work.

In other words, the priest cannot take a lack of receptivity on the part of those to whom he speaks as evidence that he, the priest, is either ineffective or lacking the presence of Christ in his vocation.

This is important, particularly during this time when so many do not serve. I see that some priests are discouraged and do not proceed with an awareness of their value to each of us, a value which has eternal consequences. The fact that people do not recognize the truth is no reason to stop speaking the truth because someday, with God's grace and when they are ready, these people will think back to the words of the priest and they will recognize these words as truth.

One who sows seeds must be content to leave the seeds to germinate at the correct time. It is for the farmer to reap the harvest and Jesus Christ Himself will collect the harvest at the appropriate time for each soul.

Priests must always look to Christ and His experience on earth. Did Christ always feel effective in His teaching and preaching?

Well, after Christ spoke the truth to Pilate, the people crucified Him. Does this mean Christ was ineffective and His service and suffering pointless and fruitless? Clearly not.

In the same way, often a priest will be denied immediate gratification in terms of witnessing the fruits of his labor, just as Christ, in His humanity, did not live to see what His three years of preaching and ultimate death on the cross would achieve. The priest, at ordination, agrees to share in this service and sacrifice and accepts that, unlike an earthly bridge builder, he will not usually see the end result of his work until he reaches eternity.

This is all the more reason why the eternity of each priest will delight us. We will then certainly see the bridges built by each priest. We will see the elaborate benefits and interconnecting graces that pulled many of us back into the safety net of the family of God or that protected many of us from falling out of the safety net of the family of God. Indeed, only then will we see the intricate safety nets woven for us by each priest in his daily "yes" to Jesus Christ. How their constant labors represent God's love for each of us and how their daily service speaks to us of God's love present in each one of them. Oh, dear. It is so very clear that we do not love them enough.

In heaven, we will be filled with awe at the power of goodness that the Lord allowed to burst into the world in each daily Mass.

In heaven, we will see the spectacular healings that took place through the Sacrament of Confession and the great calm that washed over anguished souls at the encounters with Christ they experienced through the Anointing of the Sick.

How grateful we will be in heaven when we witness what happened in our moment of Baptism and at our Confirmations.

At the other end of each of these experiences is a man, serving in his humanity.

Truly, each priestly act will be part of that priest's eternity and we will rejoice with each priest and for each priest at the reward he enjoys for his service to the kingdom.

I have often said that many priests underestimate the influence and impact they have on those they serve. For Catholics, the priestly presence is knitted into the most pivotal experiences of our lives.

Consider our First Holy Communion, Confirmation, Marriage, the Baptism of our children, the death of our loved ones, our own deaths. These life-changing moments are presided over by Christ through a priest. People remember with such gratitude the presence of the priest at the bedside of a dying family member and at their funerals. People, often in brokenness, look to the priest to make sense out of some of the tragic circumstances experienced during our time on earth.

Far from feeling unable or unequal to the task, the priest should accept that he, in his humanity, could disappoint, but

Christ, in His divinity, will never disappoint. In other words, to repeat an important thought, the priest can rejoice and be at peace in the limitations of his humanity while constantly proclaiming the power of Christ's divinity.

Our Lady said that we are giving her the greatest pleasure by illuminating the divine presence of her Son in each priestly vocation. Our Lady is devoted to each of her children but she pays special attention to the needs of God's beloved priests.

I see that each priest is different as each man is different. Their unique character is designed by God for the service He requires from them. God takes all of their attributes and, with the most gentle tap of a divine touch, sanctifies them.

If a priest desires holiness, he must turn inward, to Jesus Christ in his soul.

The flame of divine love burns steadily in each priest. The more a priest turns his eyes inward, to Christ, the greater the amount of God's love that can flow through him.

We are each this way, of course. The more we climb our mountain of holiness, the more effectively Christ can use us.

There is something different about the priesthood, though. The mark of Jesus Christ, or shall we call it the stamp of the First Priest, predisposes the man to becoming transformed into another Christ. In order to cooperate with this transformation, a priest has to desire to be like Christ. I do not believe that every man ordained necessarily possesses a passionate desire for this transformation. I believe that this desire can come and grow and become compelling as the priest comes to know Christ through his ministry or through his suffering and sacrifice, or indeed through whatever circumstances God allows for him. God Himself will fuel this desire for transformation, particularly when He is asked.

Transformation, by its nature, demands change. St. Paul

speaks to this.

"It is no longer I who live, but Christ who lives in me" (Gal 2:20).

This is the goal. This transformation from one man, the priest, to another, Christ, requires that one of the two participants must change. Clearly, Jesus Christ who is God cannot change. It is not even possible. So it is the man who must change. The priest has to constantly reduce his will, making it smaller and smaller until it disappears altogether. You might say that this transformation is actually a process of reduction. The priest in his daily "yes" to Jesus cooperates with the shrinking of his human will. John the Baptist knew this.

"He must increase but I must decrease" (John 3:30).

Yes, the human will in each priest has to go when it does not match the divine will. It, self-will, must be jettisoned, sacrificed to the process of unity with Christ in service to the Father for the good of the Body of Christ and for God's greater glory. Only the will of the Father should remain for the man to be authentically Jesus Christ.

If this process, this transformation, were to rely on the priest, it would not even be worth embarking upon, so obviously impossible would it both appear and actually be. But this process relies on Jesus Christ.

The priest must allow himself to be grafted to the vine that is Christ.

"I am the true vine, and My Father is the vinedresser...Abide in Me, and I in you. As the branch cannot bear fruit by itself, unless it abides in the vine, neither can you, unless you abide in Me. I am the vine, you are the branches. He who abides in Me, and I in him, he it is that bears much fruit, for apart from Me you can do nothing" (John 15:1, 4-5).

Consider please that the act of allowing oneself to be grafted to the will of another is heroic, all by itself. It is an acknowledgement by a man that alone he is of less value than he will be if he is attached to the divine. This acknowledgement, when made with honesty, is a lovely and sublime act of humility that enables Christ to begin the transformation. You might say, actually, that this acknowledgement is the beginning of the transformation.

Pride is the enemy of this acknowledgement, of course, but this is not a work on pride, but on the power of Jesus Christ to transform and as the self-will diminishes, so does the pride.

We ask God constantly for the discernment to identify His will, then reduce our will and replace it with the divine will. That is the daily goal, the ongoing cooperation with the process of transformation.

I understand that God's priests are called to this process in a profound way. I do not have words to distinguish the call to holiness that is the priest's from that of a lay person or even a female religious, but I know that there is something here that, like Our Lady's role, is distinct. I am in no way minimizing the heroic call to holiness of others. I am simply concentrating in this moment on the call to the priesthood.

A priest offers his whole life for service to us, God's children. How many of us look to Jesus and say, "Take my life, Lord. Use it. I am willing to sacrifice myself so that my brothers and sisters might know You and be saved?"

This is what a priest gives to God for us, his whole life.

Brothers and sisters, this is a complete sacrifice. Jesus, always mindful of nourishing the Body of Christ, accepts each of these offerings with indescribable reverence and hope. He understands that the man who offers himself to the priesthood is giving everything in the name of the Invisible Reality. This is such a big offering. Can we take it in at all? Possibly not. Possibly this will require the divine vision that is available to us only after we die in our bodies.

I am at peace with the inability to understand the scope of this offering but our limited understanding should not prevent us from marveling at and seeking to protect each vocation to the priesthood.

To make another point about the Lord's experience of an offering made by a man of his life in the priesthood, I view it from a different angle. I believe that when a man is ordained, when he enters this covenant, Jesus understands completely where the man experiences weakness. Jesus understands completely where the man is likely to trip and fall. Jesus sees both the strengths and the weaknesses in the man and Jesus provides the priest with His own kind of safety net. Jesus will literally wrap the priest in protection so that he does not do damage. The priest accepts this protection by committing to prayer and a disciplined prayer life. If the priest denies Jesus access, in other words, does not pray, Jesus is limited in the amount of protection He can give the priest and the priest is then more likely to do damage to the goals of God.

Now we must be clear that when Jesus acts through the priest in a sacramental way, heaven's goals are protected. The priest need not be particularly holy or indeed even in the state of grace for the validity of the sacrament performed by and through the priest. What I am saying is that if a priest is connected to Christ through prayer and silence, through a willingness to reduce his human will and replace it with the Lord's will, that priest will be better able to express and distribute God's mercy and love in his service. It can be no other way and the love of the First Priest will be communicated to others through each successive priest.

To be even more clear, I will say it this way. Others have told me that they can only confess to one priest because only this one priest understands them. I accept that certain personalities work well together and I accept that the methods of one priest may appeal to a given person more than the methods of another. At the same time, if I needed to have my Confession heard, I would go to any priest in complete confidence, regardless of the apparent condition of the priest.

The Lord is present in each priest. Each of us can trust in His presence.

To make a final point on this, most of us, priests included, have been exposed to priests who speak and act against the teaching of the Church. Clearly, if a priest is exhorting others to be disobedient to the Church or Church teaching, or if a priest himself is behaving sinfully or in a way that is disobedient to Church teaching, we can be sure that we are dealing with the self-will of the priest and not the divine will. Even in these cases, though, the sacraments performed by the priest are valid and the sacramental graces present.

I see that Jesus loves His priests most tenderly. His plan for renewal rests in the hearts of His priests.

If Jesus Christ wills a renewal for the world, and He does, a renewal will occur. Each of us must determine our individual role in the renewal with a great determination to serve to the fullest possible extent, thereby maximizing the Lord's reach through our individual commitment.

When we are beginning to serve to a fuller extent, giving the Lord a more total "yes," we will feel stretched. Jesus calls us to surpass our intended line of service and step out into the unknown with Him. There is often a temptation to remain safely within what is comfortable for us but this is not good and we should be alert to this natural human proclivity. We will be comfortable in heaven for eternity, after all. We must accept some discomfort during our time on earth.

I would urge priests to rejoice in God's presence. Rejoice in God's plan. Each priest must strive to rejoice in God's choosing of him for such glorious service to the kingdom, even though that service is often cloaked in the most humble of tasks. The call to rejoicing is an imperative for priests because only through rejoicing can they proclaim Christ with any accuracy.

Some might question whether or not rejoicing is possible in a time when the Church is suffering so badly in many areas. But Christ has not abandoned His Church. Christ is truly present in each one of us who loves Him. Heaven has not changed. There is great rejoicing in heaven and there is great rejoicing on earth by anyone who is connected to the Lord in his soul.

God's kingdom comes and rejoicing is in order.

Each priest must look honestly into his soul. In his soul, he will find the eyes of Christ. When one meets the divine gaze, one is strengthened and confirmed in service. A priest makes a commitment to an Invisible Reality, that is, Jesus Christ truly present in his ministry. Well, it is abundantly clear then that Jesus Christ must be *allowed* to be truly present in the ministry of each priest.

Fathers, increase your prayer time. Nourish your prayer life. Scrutinize your personal relationship with the Lord because it is only through this relationship that rejoicing can occur.

Rejoice. Proclaim.

The priest must connect himself to Jesus Christ and rejoice in the Lord's presence. We are called to bring Good News, not bad news. The world brings bad news to God's children in a steady flow. We, who are called to be different, must accept personally that God has not left us and that God has a need for fidelity in this time as He does in every other time.

We will move from an Age of Disobedience to an Age of

Obedience and we will do this through one person at a time. God's beloved priests will set an example of obedience, both in thought and action.

When one is being attacked unjustly, there is a temptation to respond in a defensive way, with anger. This is human nature. We, as followers of Christ, must reject our human nature and respond with God's divine nature. We must try to rest in God's truth, refusing to become discouraged by the fact that falseness appears to abound. The first apostles were consistently persecuted.

"We are in difficulties on all sides, but never cornered; we see no answer to our problems, but never despair; we have been persecuted, but never deserted; knocked down, but never killed; always, wherever we may be, we carry with us in our body the death of Jesus, so that the life of Jesus, too, may always be seen in our body" (Corinthians 4:8-10).

Yes, it is clear that the early apostles struggled. It is also clear, though, that they expected no less. They understood that if they were called to follow Jesus they would be treated like Jesus, whose experience included mockery and anguish.

"So they went on their way from the presence of the Council, rejoicing that they had been considered worthy to suffer shame for His name. And every day in the temple and from house to house, they kept right on teaching and preaching Jesus as the Christ" (Acts 5: 41-42).

The priesthood is being attacked in this time, both directly and indirectly. There is no shortage of ignorance from those who seek to avoid God's will in their own lives. In many areas, this has created for priests an atmosphere where it is difficult to rejoice and proclaim.

Beloved Fathers of God's children, the enemy offers shame

and bitterness from this purification, it is true. But at the same time, God offers humility and gentleness. We are not bound to accept the ugly fruits of the enemy's efforts. We can reject despair and feelings of futility.

We are bound instead to accept the bountiful fruits of the renewal. If we do so, we will never be trapped in helplessness by the shocking pain of the sins committed by the few.

We must rejoice in God's presence and allow the Lord to bring healing and renewal to each of us personally. Jesus will do this for each of us. Truly, I am certain that each priest will experience a burst of joy if He asks for it.

This renewal, this commitment to personal transformation, will produce humility and great heavenly calm. Christ will possess each priestly vocation to a degree that will delight each priest, creating an invulnerable protection against the temptations of the times.

Truly, God's desire to renew the priesthood is passionate.

When one feels passionate about something, one very often gives to a degree that appears to exceed common thinking and expectation.

I believe God is passionately committed to a renewal of holiness in His priests. Today's priests must be equally passionate about abandoning themselves to the cause of the Church. They must be as committed as the first apostles.

The combination of God's passionate desire to renew the priesthood with the priest's passionate commitment to proclaiming Christ will draw the renewal down into the world like nothing else.

Rejoice in God's presence. Proclaim His presence to the world.

Mary, our mother, is available to us in each moment. She

serves faithfully with Jesus, calling out most particularly to priests. She watches, ever vigilant, for every opportunity to protect and defend each priest. She, in her feminine way, makes available to each priest an example of gentle nurturing, the same nurturing that she uses with each of her children.

It seems to me that Our Lady was granted union with God here on earth and as such there was no wrenching process necessary for her to move from humanity to eternity. This was a sublime graciousness on the part of God. He bestowed all that heaven had to offer on her. For Our Lady, the heavenly union was achieved, through her willingness and cooperation and through God's great graciousness, on earth. We all experience union with Christ in heaven in the same way that Our Lady experiences union with Christ in heaven but she is different.

I am not saying Our Lady is divine. For clarity let me say that I see this as a vision. Our Lady was conceived mystically in the heart of the Father. From that heart, she proceeded into the world. Her heart never separated from God's heart. When it was time, He glanced at her. She knew Him immediately in this mystical way and accepted His Son, God, into her body as a human mother but also into her soul as one who experiences union in heaven. So at the moment of the Lord's physical conception, the Incarnation, Our Lady became like one who enters heaven. She achieved union, through necessity and desire on God's part, and willingness and longing on her part, like the saint who is taken up into permanent residence in heaven. Only she remained on earth. As a concession and reward and as a way of making her stand out as God's human temple, God brought her into heaven at the end of her life just the way she was, in this perpetual spiritual union.

I don't know how to clarify this except to say that Our Lady stands out as God's chosen Queen of heaven and earth. This is huge. Who is above her? Only the Trinity. Her role will never be repeated. As such, she would merit very close study.

Every time I talk about Our Lady, I come to the priesthood. It is like an intellectual cul de sac for me. I think I am trying to distinguish between Our Lady's union with God and God's presence in the priesthood.

Our Lady had perfect purity. Priests serving in their humanity do not. God's giving the priest a share of His divinity at ordination is something different from what Our Lady experienced and yet I believe it is comparable in many ways. I see a similarity between what happened to Mary at the Incarnation and what happens to a priest at Ordination.

I believe it was very important for God to show us how to live. It was for this reason He sent Christ. He sent Christ as the ideal for humanity in male form. I believe Our Lady is the ideal for humanity in female form. While she was not perfect as God is perfect, she perfectly represents God's presence in a woman. Just as we all, both men and women, should strive to be like Jesus in character and behavior, we should also strive to be like Mary in character and behavior.

I believe Mary must be God's most favored servant. She is the Saint Among Saints, the epitome of the servant of God. Many saints have bestowed upon them by God high levels of unity or even union while they remain on earth.

I believe with great certainty that none compare to Mary.

A priest who studies the gentleness and obedience of Mary will make great gains in the authentic representation of her Son.

Almighty God,
Father of our Lord Jesus Christ,
to You I pledge my allegiance
and the service of my entire life.
Grant me the help of Your Spirit
to live like Mary, my Mother,
in perfect obedience to Your holy will.
Amen.

Prayer written by a priest for priests.

Part Six

Monthly Messages from
Jesus Christ

Jesus

Be at peace, little children of God. I am with you. Do not think that you are orphans, abandoned to a world which lacks God's love. I seek to bring love into the world in a continuous stream. How My little apostles delight Me with their willingness to allow Me to use them for this purpose. I work without pause in each soul that welcomes Me. You may be asleep, or at rest in another way, and I am busy at work in your soul, preparing great gifts for your brothers and sisters who do not know Me. I am tireless. I am determined. I am forming many saints who will move up the mountain of holiness with speed in order to serve Me more completely. Do you wish to be one of these saints? Of course you do. We will work together, you and I, to move you more fully into My will. How I guard My little apostles. How I surround them with My protection. I watch your life closely so that every experience you have will benefit your soul. My little ones experience pain and carry wounds. This should not frighten you. I do not judge you for your pain. I look at your pain and remember My pain and I am compassionate. Your pain will not separate you from Me. Again I say, have no fear. I am working in your soul to bring My kingdom to earth through you. I will see to everything. Trust your Jesus and you will be at peace.

Jesus

August 1, 2006

I send My apostles the grace necessary for a calm spirit. With this calm spirit, My followers will bring heavenly calm to a restless world that trembles with unease. Live your commitment to time spent in silent prayer and I will place these heavenly graces in your soul. Others will identify these graces in you because these gifts are contrary to the gifts offered by the world. This is another way that My apostles stand out. Do not spend a great deal of time discussing events in the world. Long discussions do not benefit the situation. Spend instead a great deal of time praying for the situation in the world. This will benefit the situation, along with those around you, and your own little priceless soul, which becomes more and more beautiful through prayer and silence. I want each apostle to understand that I have not abandoned this world. Consider this carefully. I am Jesus. I am God. I have not abandoned this world. Do not be afraid. I say this, dearest apostles, firmly. I do not want My apostles to be afraid or to communicate fear to others. Bring your fears to Me and bring My peace to others. This is your call, your divine task. Accept this call as seriously as you accept My love for you and your love for Me. Our reciprocal love is natural and right, holy and blessed. My peace in your soul is also natural and right, holy and blessed. Apostles, be disciplined in

197

those actions that bring you peace and be equally disciplined in avoiding those things that cause you upset. Your Jesus seeks to comfort many. Very often, I will do this through you.

Jesus

September 1, 2006

A deep peace settles upon those who serve the Lord. This interior peace, heaven's presence, connects each apostle to their Savior. I work in each soul without interruption if that soul welcomes Me. Around the apostle, circumstances change. Others come and go in their life and perhaps there is suffering or persecution. My presence remains a constant, though, comforting, consoling, and directing. The connection between heaven and each apostolic servant is the avenue through which I return to the world. How heaven delights in each commitment. During this time many look to their Savior with a certainty that I am calling out to them. Each apostle hears My call. You have heard My call. Consider today what your Jesus is asking of you. Consider how I am asking you to serve today. Dearest apostle, I must insist that you spend time in silence contemplating My will. I must insist upon this because I require your service in whatever way I have willed for you during this time. If you give Me your full attention for a period of time each day, I can instruct you and prompt you. Also, I can give you a very important heavenly attribute and that is the peace that I need you to possess. You must possess this for your own comfort, of course, but you must also possess this peace so that it flows through you into the world. Your world does not have peace. My peace has been rejected by your world. You, My beloved apostles, reject the world's discord and accept My peace. That is why you are so important to Me. I am your Beloved One. You feel My presence, do you not? Truly, I am with you. Dear apostle, I want to be with everyone in this way. Will you help Me? I know that you will. Spend time with Me in silence each day and I will provide you with everything you need and everything the world requires.

Jesus

My children, I am with you. Your God, your Creator, speaks this message in so many ways. In every daybreak you must hear My voice saying, "I am with you." When tempted toward despair because of crosses and hardships, you must hear My whisper saying, "I am with you." When you look at the work you must do and find it overwhelming, allow me to move you gently into it with perfect assurance that 'I am with you.' Dearest apostles, so brave, I am with you. I do not tell you that you will be overcome. I do not tell you that you have been given work that is impossible for you to complete. Those messages do not come from Me. Instead, I tell you that you will persevere and ultimately triumph. Our mission of mercy does not falter, even though the steps of my little apostles sometimes falter. This mission pushes through the world with a steadiness that defies all attempts against it. My apostles experience fear at times. This is not a problem for Me or this mission. Fear is to be expected. Bring your fear to Me and explain to Me exactly what threatens you. If you do this, I can remove your fear. I will convince you that in My presence, with My power, everything is possible. You have an expectation of your little boat crashing against the rocks. I will never allow this. If I am steering the boat that is your work, you will be carried safely. Push on into each day with courage, understanding that while you may not be able, I am able. You may lack courage, but I have courage. You sometimes walk in darkness, but I have the light with which to see exactly where your footsteps are taking you. Dear apostles, it is a time for hard work, yes, but a time for great glory, also. Rejoice. I am with you.

Jesus

I am real, dear apostles. Do not worry that you have misplaced your trust. You will be rewarded for your service and commitment. The wise apostle understands that he has already been rewarded, of course. The wise apostle understands that being close to the King as a trusted servant is a reward in itself because through the proximity to the King, the servant becomes more and more noble. I am changing you if you are walking with Me. I am stretching your spiritual capabilities. My beloved lay apostles will find that the changes in their soul are constant, but gentle. There is great spiritual progress available in this time. This is My mercy and this is My plan. Through the holiness of the few, I will convert many. Be courageous while I make these changes in your soul. Be at peace. The Savior seeks to preserve His plan by calling more and more into the field of service. Rejoice when you see many responding. Understand that this plan is for all. You are called. You are listening to My direction and you are becoming holier. Through you, I call to others. Others listen and respond, and through them, I call out again, to more and more. In this way, a multitude is drawn into the safety of the family of God. Be at peace, little apostle. All is well and heaven is content that God's plan is proceeding. I will never leave you to execute My plan alone. You will al-

*ways be acting with Me if you are acting for Me.
Do you understand? I know that you understand
because it is simple. I am with you. I will never
leave you.*

Jesus

December 1, 2006

I speak with determination today. I look at My lay apostles, serving so diligently to prepare others for My return, and I am consoled. My heart sighs with the rejection of some but also lifts in hope at the acceptance of so many. Little apostles, you are pleasing to Me. You are laboring for heaven and you are teamed with heaven. Together, we are bringing hope to those who were formerly without hope. This is the way for you, the path to holiness. I direct you in everything and you proceed along this path that I have marked out for you. All is well in your case. I want to explain to you why I speak with determination today. I am determined to push out further into the world. I desire that everyone have the light of heaven. I want confidence for all and comfort for anyone suffering. I send a great rush of grace for conversions at this time. This is a time for hearts to change. Because I desire this, a great many conversions, I am supplying all that is necessary to achieve this goal. You will find, My apostles, that many will be drawn to the truth of your mission. Accept this with profound humility. Show the world how small you are and they will see how great I am. This is the way to win souls for the Father. I am so pleased when an apostle accepts slights and insults with peace. I am pleased by this because it shows Me that you are truly ac-

cepting the call to imitate Me. It also shows Me that arrogance is receding and humility is spreading. Oh, what joy this gives to the infant in the manger. Accepting insults in humility is a most favorable gift for the King. Truly, I look at these offerings and I rejoice. When I rejoice, graces flow unhindered and unencumbered, bathing the whole world. Never underestimate the power of you, the humble apostle, joined to Me, the determined God. Together, we are changing the world.

Jesus

I, Jesus, take delight in My apostles. I look into the world and see My friends, serving each other and growing in love, and truly I experience delight. My friends, you will be well rewarded. The holier you become, the easier it will be for you to come to heaven. That is My goal for you, that you become so holy on earth that your death be a time of great peace and joy. How I anticipate the homecoming of each of My beloved servants. I plan for the day and prepare for the great rejoicing that will take place. You will be welcomed into eternity by a multitude of apostles, all of whom served before you. You will recognize your friends and family in heaven and they will assemble to greet you. Such joyous reunion. Such well-earned reward. My friends, your life will pass quickly, far more quickly than you can imagine. I speak to you today to remind and encourage you. I remind you that you are committed to Me, to My will. Begin each day remembering that you have made a commitment to serve heaven on that day. If you pledge your allegiance to God, you are on the side of God. If you are on the side of God, you are working against God's enemy. I want you to reject all that comes from the enemy. Be diligent about your time in silence and I will reveal anything that I wish you to reject or abandon. I draw you into My heart, further and further. There is always a need to advance. Today, I call you to make an even greater commitment to advancing in holiness. I will help you, of course. I will make your path even more clear to you. I come today to remind you of your pledge, but also to encourage you. I look into the world at this time and there is darkness, it is true, but there is also light and that light comes from your commitment to Me. The angels see your service and they rejoice. The saints see your service and they applaud. Our mother, Mary, sees your service and she is comforted. I, Jesus Christ, see your service and I experience delight. You are part of a team, My team. We are the team that brings salvation and we do that through love. In your heart I am placing a love for humanity. You will experience this love individually, for each person with whom you come in contact. This is how I experience love. I love all mankind and I do this one person at a time. You must do the same. Love those around you, particularly those in your family. Treat each person with dignity and respect because if people see that you are good, they will understand that I am good. Be at peace. I am with you in everything and your service delights Me.

Jesus

February 1, 2007

My little apostles continue to grow in holiness. Today, I call you to obedience. It is My desire that you examine your life and bring obedience into each area. I will help you. Is there an area where you can improve? Do you wish Me to illuminate this for you? Consider with Me, your Savior, where you can do better. There are concrete areas, of course, but there are also areas where it is the spirit of obedience that is lacking and by this I mean the spirit of love and humility. Do not think so much of the condition of other souls. Concentrate instead on the condition of your own soul. In consideration of obedience, it is good to think like a small child. A small child, one who is loved by his parents, seeks to be good and pleasing. His goodness and small acts of obedience enable him to feel good about himself and the path of purity that he is choosing. Some of my little ones in the world have lost this innocence. I want this for you. It is this innocence that will admit you to heaven, after all. Together we must cultivate it. Separate worldly opinion from My opinion because the world will tell you that you are foolish to be obedient in small matters, for example, if nobody is noticing you. But I am always with you and I notice you in each moment. Look at each situation, regardless of how seemingly unimportant, and try to be obedient. You do not do this alone, but with

Me, because together we work on your spiritual growth. It is our job, yours and mine. It is our project. It is an interesting and joyful project to Me. I love nothing better than helping you to improve the condition of your soul. As your soul's condition improves, you learn more and more about Me and how much I love you. Do you want to learn more about how much I love you? Practice obedience in small things. I do not expect you to become perfect at once. Do not expect this of yourself. Be gentle with yourself. I love you so much that I do not want you to judge yourself harshly. In the same way, I will never be harsh with you. I will never be hard or cold. You are cherished, my beloved one. I am your Jesus, always here for you. Take My hand and I will lead you closer to obedience each day.

Jesus

March 1, 2007

My beloved apostles, how hard you are working. How diligently you see to My desires. I am bringing you to holiness, slowly and gently, but certainly. Your course leads you to My heart and in each moment of each day you are drawn more fully to Me. You may not feel the increase in holiness. You may not notice your progress but be assured that progress is being made. Your holiness blossoms under the prudent and watchful care of the Divine Gardner. You may wish to advance more quickly. You may sigh at the labors necessary for advancing in holiness. I understand both of these things but I tell you today that you should not be discouraged. It is I, Jesus, after all, who contemplates your soul and determines the speed with which you need to progress to arrive at the perfect place at the correct time. If you were to move too quickly, you might miss this mark. If you were to stop laboring, you would not advance as far as I require. Be at peace in the place where you are spiritually and understand that I am ministering to you constantly there. Be also at peace that you must labor for holiness, moving constantly forward in virtue. I am with you. I take your willingness to serve and your willingness to become holier and truly I flow great things into your soul and into the world. I ask that each apostle find quiet during this time, allowing silence to prune the weeds that spring up in each day's activity. We work together on your soul, as I have said, and I, Jesus, expect that there is work to be done. If I did not expect that your soul needed work, I would say that you had advanced far enough and I would take you to heaven. When you see the condition of your soul and you correctly identify that there is work to be done and projects to undertake, rejoice. Compare your soul to My soul and you will see a glimpse of the completion of this project. You must say, "Truly, I trust that Jesus will get me there if I follow Him." I will not abandon the project of your holiness. Neither should you. The personal holiness of each apostle is given My greatest attention because each project in the world flows from this project in individual souls. Do you understand? Are you at peace with this? I need you to become holier each day so that I can become more present in the world each day. If you are new to the walk to holiness, rejoice. You are welcome and you will flourish. If you have been walking toward holiness for many years, rejoice. You are valued and you are making progress. Through you, I renew the world. Rejoice. My plan for you and for the world is well underway.

Jesus

My beloved apostles rest in My heart each time they pray. Truly, when you come to Me, I am there. There are times when you feel abandoned as I felt abandoned. I allow this so that you can share My experience. In this way, by sharing My experience of abandonment, you come to know Me more completely. Through this intimacy you become more like Me. My dear ones, it is through sharing My experiences that you learn to love others who carry crosses. There are times when your humanity leads you to judge another but because you have suffered, you offer compassion instead of condemnation. Each experience in your life, shared with Me, increases your holiness and your capacity for compassion. Think of the times when someone treated you with compassion when you expected condemnation. Think of the times in your life when someone treated you with kindness and support, overlooking a failure or a flaw. My friends, you do not always understand but it is the crosses you carry that enhance these heavenly capabilities in your soul. I know you struggle. I accept your weaknesses. Do not think that your anguish is a measure of your holiness. Do not think that because you find your cross heavy, you are not making progress. I am with you and I am advancing you, even while you groan with weariness. The kingdom will make the best possible use of the inevitable suffering that accompanies your humanity. Your decision to serve is all that is necessary to draw graces for others from your life. Be at peace that I understand your suffering and your movement to holiness. I am with you in each moment. I take the greatest joy in accepting your suffering and rewarding it with heavenly gains, both in your soul and in the world. You are My beloved ones. You are My chosen ones. The greatest care is taken with each of your little souls. Your progress is apparent from My vantage point. You must trust Me and allow Me to access others through you. Think back on our walk together. Think of the great graces I have flowed through you in the past. This flow of grace is increasing by the moment and is not dependant on your perfection but on My perfection. My presence in your soul brings a perfume into the world that is irreplaceable. I need you. Our unity, yours and Mine, brings unique benefits to the kingdom. Yes, you are important to Me and to your heavenly family. Rest against your Jesus now as I send you courage and strength and heavenly calm.

Jesus

May 1, 2007

My apostles, I speak to you with such hope. Why do I feel hope when I speak these words? I, your Jesus, feel hope because you are reading these words and listening to Me. In your soul, you are interested in My plan. In your soul you are willing to make the changes which will bring about My plan. In your soul you receive a foretaste of heaven which provides you with the joy that I wish to make available to others. My heavenly plan is truly rooted in your soul and for this reason I have hope. The times in which you live provide you with opportunities to practice hope, even while much of the world feels dismay and fear. My apostles see that the world is changing and this is the message, a message of hope, which flows through them. You are precious to Me, both because of the unique love I have for you and for the unique plan I have for you. Allow Me to rest in your soul each day and I will fill you with My love. Where can you find more silence? How can you give your Jesus just a few more minutes of time to be with you and sanctify you even further? My beloved apostle, please be disciplined about your time with Me in each day. I do not want you to be distracted. I do not want the world to take your hope from you. If you do not spend time with Me, you are vulnerable to the fears sowed by the enemy of hope. I rely on My beloved ones. In them I find rest and solace. You see, dear apostle, if I can change you and fill you with My great spiritual blessings, I can change others. Is there even one life that you can say you affected by your faith in Me and by My presence in you? Do not limit My plan in your mind. My plan is vast and it is working. Be joyful today as I am joyful. Hope in Me, dear one, as I hope in you. Trust in Me as I trust in you. Be with Me as I long to be with you and together we will fill the world with hope, drawing many wounded souls back into our family of love.

Jesus

June 1, 2007

Heavenly consideration is the compass which will insure a true course for each apostle. In every situation, consider heaven's goals for you and for those around you. The apostle who gives thoughtful consideration to heaven's goals will be known for speaking less, rather than more. This apostle will make decisions in My company, aware of My goals. I would ask each of My apostles to practice this today. Move into your day gently, aware that I may wish to adjust your course several times. You expect one thing, perhaps. But I, your Jesus, may need something else from you. You are committed to a certain plan, perhaps. But I, your Jesus, may have chosen a different plan altogether. Only with thoughtful consideration will you be alert to My will in each situation. Apostles, you have been prepared to serve in the manner that I require you to serve. You have been taught many things about holiness. If you are humble, you are aware that there are many things still to be learned about holiness. If you are humble, you may protest, saying, "Jesus, I am not ready. I must become holier still." I understand your weaknesses and struggles. I do not fear the limits of your humanity. I have factored your weaknesses into the plan I have for you. You should never be afraid that you lack the holiness to complete the mission that I have willed for you. I will make you holy if you proceed according to My directions. You shall have all you need. Please begin to use all that you have been taught. Begin to see others as I see others, in need of love and tolerance. You have been taught not to make judgments. Do not make judgements. You have been taught to spend time in silence. Spend time in silence. You have been taught to trust Me. Trust in Me now, today. You have been taught not to be afraid of the future. Do not fear the future. Dear apostles, you have been taught to pray. Pray. Now, today, every day. Pray. Ask Me for mercy for this world. Ask Me for conversion graces for this world. Ask Me for the Spirit of truth in such an abundance that all eyes will be opened to God's truth. My beloved faithful apostles, I want you to use everything you have been given to serve Me so that others may be saved. I am with you. I will direct you in each moment. You must be at peace so that others can learn about peace. You must be calm so that others can learn about calm. Do not underestimate the power of setting an example of heavenly consideration. It is this consideration in each apostle that will ultimately allow Me to reclaim a multitude of souls for the Father.

Jesus

I am with you. How often I repeat this. I, Jesus, am with you. I, Jesus, will never leave you. I see everything that occurs in your life. I understand exactly where your pain originates. Like nobody else, I understand you. Much of the suffering my little ones experience is from loneliness. Even if you are surrounded by others, you can feel lonely. You see, dear apostles, each person feels alone until he rests with Me. It is only after becoming united to Me that you can love each other as you were intended to love each other. There are many who do not allow unity with Me. I cannot force Myself upon them, because they are free to reject Me. But because they reject Me, they cannot love others as they were intended to love others. Others, sadly, remain unloved. Others become wounded. Others strike out in their pain, causing more distress. Humanity was created to live on earth connected to God. My apostles, even though you struggle, you remain connected to Me. I am able to heal you and send love through you. The signs of My presence are all around you, even though you struggle. Believe this. If you look at a person who has rejected Me, you will see signs of that rejection. If you look at a world that has rejected Me, you will also see signs. My beloved ones, when you see signs that God has been rejected, you must remain peaceful. I, Jesus, have told you that change is necessary. I, Jesus, have told you that I desire change. I do not abandon you and I do not abandon the world. I have many friends in this world and you are among them. You trust Me, I know. I will honor the trust you have placed in Me. I will bring all things to the good, both in your life and in the world. I, the Blameless One, have never betrayed another and I will not betray you. Think often on the promises I have made to you. I have said I will never leave you. I have said I will protect My interests in your soul. I have said I will pursue conversion of your loved ones. During this time, I want each apostle to consider these promises. Serve Me in steadiness, of course, but also, serve Me in peace. Dear apostles, you are connected to Me. You accept My love. You know that just as I cherish you, I cherish all others. My dear friends, please live these truths because others are looking to you for example. Please. Give an example of joyful trust. I need this from you so that I can draw hurting souls back to Me. I am with you. I will help you to do this.

Jesus

A small child often prays that God will help him to be good. This prayer is pleasing to God. Indeed, which prayer is more pleasing? A child prays this prayer in humility and simplicity from a pure heart seeking even greater purity. It is this purity of heart that all apostles must seek. Each day should be filled with brief prayers of this kind. If an apostle wishes to reside with the Father, that apostle must become the child of the Father. God has no equal. Do not seek greatness. Seek goodness. My beloved ones, you know that I love you and that I am grateful for your service. You know that I am pleased with your progress. Do you wonder why your Jesus calls you constantly further into holiness? Do I do this for My benefit? Yes. I do. I take great joy in seeing you advance, it is true. And yet, it is for your own personal benefit, also, that I call you to strive for higher heights. I want you to become as holy as you can. As your holiness increases, my friends, so does your peace. As your peace increases, so does the peace in this world. It is for many reasons, all similar to these, that I beckon you to come further and further into My heart. You are called to come closer to Me and move further from distractions. You turn your face toward heaven and in doing so you turn your face away from the world, which seeks to draw you away from Me. For today, pledge your alle-

giance to the Father and then strive to become holier. "Father, help me to be good." In each moment of your life there is an opportunity for goodness. Find the opportunities and try. Exert yourself, My beloved ones. Work for your holiness. If you were participating in a game, you would try to win. I want you to participate in your movement to holiness. I want you to make efforts throughout each day to choose the holiest course. I am with you in each moment, helping you. If you, My beloved apostles, will work with Me to become holier, I can reach others through you. But that is My affair. Your affair is to try to become as holy as possible. Have no fear. You are loved.

Jesus

Dear apostles, I send you a spirit of gentleness. Because you are called to treat others as I treated others, you are called to be gentle with all those around you. This call to gentleness in no way diminishes the call to live in the truth. If you preach the truth as I did, gently, you will draw others to us and to unity of thought and action. In this time, when it is so important that souls be brought back into the family of God, we must be ever so careful to be gentle with others in each interaction. I am Jesus. I am filled with love for each soul you encounter, regardless of their condition. View each person through My love and treat them with My gentleness. My dearest apostle, in order to allow yourself to heal from any wounds you yourself suffer, you must allow Me to minister to you. I am tenderhearted with your failings. Remember this and do not turn away from Me when you feel you have failed. If you do not allow Me to minister to you during periods of unrest, you will be vulnerable to the distortions which can be sown by the enemy. Apostles walking with Me inspire hope in the world. This is the plan. But My friends must remember that apostles walking with Me also inspire fear in the enemy. The enemy's fear causes him to lash out at the friends of the Returning King. Be at peace in this as it has always been this way and there is no reason for anything but con-

fidence in My plan for each day of every life. At the same time, be prepared to do battle for your holiness as I did battle. If you remain with Me, the battles will make you stronger and holier. That is My goal. Accept the gentle ministrations of your Savior in silence and you will then be an able carrier of this gentleness to others. Beloved friends, so loyal to your God, you will stand out if you are gentle and it is this that I need from you. I need you to stand out as calm and gentle representatives of the different way. The world will remember you for your gentleness if you allow Me to teach you. You are not called to change the world. I am called to change the world. You are called to represent Me accurately so that I have the opportunity with each soul you encounter. Through your love, your kindness and your gentleness, you will create heavenly opportunities for Me in the people around you. I will never miss an opportunity, I promise you. I make the best possible use of your efforts. I thank you, dear friend. Your fidelity to the Father will not be forgotten.

Jesus

October 1, 2007

My beloved apostles, please be alert to My will. At no time should you fear that I do not have a perfect plan for you. Sometimes you make decisions that are not consistent with My plan. Sometimes these decisions cause you pain and cause others pain. It is most especially at these times that you should seek Me because I will adapt My plan for you to fit your present circumstances. I am always seeking to bring you closer to Me, never more so than when you believe you have left the path through temptation or sin. When should you believe that you are on your own? Never. In which circumstances will My heart be so hardened that I will refuse to rush in with forgiveness and grace and an alternative plan for you? Such circumstances do not exist. My dearest little apostles, be assured of My willingness to work with you in each moment, regardless of your condition in that moment. In humanity, there are moments of such holiness that even heaven stops to marvel. In humanity, there are also moments of weakness and cruelty. Please believe that heaven takes the bad with the good and moves each willing soul toward greater and greater good. Heaven draws you away from temptation and away from the pain of sin. I am good, My friends, as My Father is good. You, My beloved apostles, are called to resemble Me and be good also. You strive for this, I know. Today

I ask that each apostle consider that I treated others with kindness. I have instructed you about gentleness and today I instruct you about kindness. Little apostles, the hearts of others are easily wounded. Can you remember when someone treated you unkindly? Do you remember your pain? I was treated unkindly at times and My heart felt this same pain. We do not want this for others. We want others to understand that God loves them and you, My friends, will do that when you treat them with the kindness of the Father. I will help you if you allow Me. I will teach you to remain silent in the presence of other's faults and I will teach you to speak openly about their strengths. Pause again and try to think of a kindness that was shown to you. Do you remember how you felt at that time? You felt grateful, did you not? You felt steadied. I want to flow through you to others. You will allow Me to do so if you work each day on being kind to each person you encounter. Their pain will lessen because of your kindness. The pain of the whole world will be reduced if each of My beloved apostles learns to be kind. Begin by being kind to yourself. I accept you, My friend. You must accept yourself. Be at peace in My love for you. I do not give you an instruction without also giving you the grace to carry it out so now I will teach you about kindness.

Jesus

November 1, 2007

My beloved apostle, I understand your strug-
gles. You are becoming holier and yet you do not
think you are making progress. Dear one, can you
accept that the holier you become, the more holi-
ness you crave? Can you accept that the more you
become aware of your own flaws, the more willing
you are to accept flaws in others? I am at peace
that you are coming to know Me better. Each day
brings growth of some kind for you, even if that
growth originates in mistakes acknowledged and
corrected. I understand you, dear apostle. I know
that on some days you are ready for the battle of
holiness and that on some days you feel you are
not strong enough for the battle. This is what I
want to tell you. You rise each day and pledge
your allegiance to the Father. This commitment of
your day insures that your Father takes you each
day in the condition He finds you. Each weakness
is used to increase your humility and illuminate
for you the path to transformation. Do not become
discouraged by the need for improvement. If you
but continue on the path you have embarked
upon, you will experience greater holiness. It can
be no other way because those who pledge alle-
giance to the Father are cared for in every detail.
Our greatest goal for you is holiness because only
in holiness will you find peace and joy. Look
around you. How many have committed them-

selves to holiness as you have committed yourself to holiness? If you look at others, you will see that the Savior can count only a few as His committed apostles. And yet, every person, regardless of their condition, longs for the holiness you seek, even if their longing is denied and ignored. My heart is moved to such pity for those who do not seek Me. Let your heart also be moved to pity. Show constant compassion, never judgment, to those who do not understand what they lack. I am trying to show you, My beloved apostle, that you have begun a journey that must be taken by each person who will spend eternity in the family of God. If others delay the journey, that is their affair. My beloved apostles understand that this journey, the journey to holiness, is the most important journey they will ever take. This is your first priority, My friends. Continue to make your pledge and I will see to it that you become holier.

Jesus

December 1, 2007

We are a faith of waiting. You wait for Me to return to the world and I wait for souls to return to Me. You feel a longing for Me and for goodness that causes you pain at times. I feel a similar longing for souls in the world who have rejected Me and so suffer the pain of separation from Me. How they hurt. How their wounds disturb them and cause them to hurt others. My heart sighs with loneliness for them. I ache to comfort them and console them. I long to heal their wounds. You, My beloved apostles, comfort Me in this grief by sharing this experience with Me. I am comforted by your fidelity to Me which is reflected in your fidelity to the cause of your brothers and sisters. As I wait, so do you wait and as I suffer, so do you suffer. I speak to you today, though, to remind you of something. As I rejoice, so should you rejoice. Rejoice with Me at the return of many souls just as perhaps others rejoiced at your return. Rejoice with Me at the healing of many souls, just as perhaps others rejoiced at your healing. You will rejoice that others return to Me through your consistent and humble service. We are a faith of waiting, it is true, but we are also a faith of rejoicing. The Father's goodness spreads out over the earth in this time in waves of kindness and benevolence. You, My beloved apostles, gently push these waves out with your commitment to My service. The great mercy of the Father draws souls to My heart, the heart that burns steadily, a furnace of divine compassion and love. We are waiting, yes. But while we are waiting, we are preparing. You prepare to receive your King and I prepare to receive the fruits of your service. Be at peace, My beloved friends. We serve together, we suffer together, and we rejoice together. Be assured that you are loved and that your loneliness is temporary. I am returning.

Jesus

January 1, 2008

I am always with you, dear apostles. You move through your days of service learning greater and greater lessons in holiness. I am the teacher. When you offer Me your day, you pledge to remain with Me throughout it. This in no way diminishes the need for you to experience your humanity with all of its joys and sorrows. On the contrary, it is through your daily joys and sorrows that you are learning the lessons of love. You might think that your cross is heavy and perhaps in truth the cross that you carry is heavy. You might think that you would proceed more easily or more swiftly without the cross. This is possible, My friends, but to what purpose? Surely, I, Jesus Christ, could have advanced more quickly and comfortably to Calvary without the jeering of the crowds, the physical infirmities or the weight of the cross. This is an obvious statement. But you were destined to be saved by My Passion. The whole world benefited by My decision to accept God's will, which included suffering. In the same way, the world is benefiting from your decision to accept the crosses in your life. You offer Me your day. This is such a simple thing from the eyes of the world and yet, from the eyes of heaven, this is a very large offering indeed. Do not be afraid of the cross in each day. Do not think that your cross will interfere with the plan that I have for you. The truth is the

231

opposite. The plan that I have for you includes suffering, and your holiness will increase because of your crosses. I do not rejoice in the suffering of My friends. No, I do not. I do rejoice in the willingness of My friends to suffer, for Me and with Me. This will never change. My gratitude toward each of My beloved apostles increases as each day's commitment flows into the past. A stream of allegiance pledges trail behind you as you proceed into tomorrow. Be at peace in your crosses, I beg you, because your crosses benefit you in ways that you cannot understand. It must be enough for you that the Savior understands. If you are weary, do not be afraid. You will have what you require to cope and I will sustain you. I was weary, also. If you falter, do not be discouraged. I faltered, also, and I will lift you back to your feet. There are no circumstances that should cause you to be anxious because just as you pledge your allegiance to the Father, I, the Savior, pledge My allegiance to you. I will take care of you, My beloved ones. You will not be abandoned.

Jesus

My friend, heaven has accomplished many things with your service to the kingdom. Shall I tell you what we are achieving together? First of all, we have increased your holiness. It is true, dear apostle. With your cooperation, I have been able to advance you in virtue. Consider where you were in the holiness walk when you first committed to serving as My apostle. Consider where you are now. You will see that you have advanced, even though you also see that you have additional work to do in this regard. I want you to understand, though, that progress has been made so that you will rejoice and have hope for additional progress. This is good for you and good for heaven. Next, your service to the kingdom has been used to bring light to other souls. Think for a moment. Is it not true that you have tried to treat others more like I treated others? Is it not true that there have been times when you returned love for hostility? Have you not discovered that you view even your enemies with greater compassion? Think dear apostles. Have you shared My merciful message with others? Have they benefited? Without your cooperation, this could not have happened. Yes, many have benefited because you have chosen to serve Me. Would you like to know of another result of your service? Heaven, as you know, is filled with perfect love and comfort.

I love all of humanity, of course, but not everyone returns My love. Because of your cooperation, I, Jesus Christ, have received a greater amount of love and comfort from your world. You, in your determination to serve Me, have bestowed upon Me the greatest consolations. The light from your willingness to serve as I wish you to serve has given Me comfort in a time when My heart aches with loneliness for so many. You have truly become My friend and I hold you in My heart most protectively. All of the intentions in your heart now move to the regular beating of My heart. I will not abandon you and I will not abandon your intentions. Together, we will see to each one of them. The loyalty you feel for your loved ones is shared by Me in that your holy desires become personal to Me as they are personal to you. Just as you are determined that your loved ones be healed, so I am determined that your loved ones be healed. These are joint projects embarked upon by the Savior and His beloved apostle. You are never alone in your concerns or your crosses. I thank you for helping heaven to accomplish so much and I will reward you, in part, by keeping the promise I have made to seek conversion of all of those dear to you. Be at peace in every trial, please, because I am with you.

Jesus

My dear friend, you will learn so much about love in heaven. You will look back at your time on earth and you will understand that many things that occurred to you were both exercises in love and opportunities to love. There is misunderstanding about love in the world but those who follow Me, My beloved apostles, seek to master love as I mastered love, in sacrifice. It is true that love creates joy. This is true. But when we take on love, it is also at times like taking on a burden which must then be carried. We should not decide for love and then, finding that love burdensome at times, set it down and walk away from it. This is not how it is done. On the contrary, if you love as I loved, you will find at times that the weight of love is heavy. I experienced this on Calvary when I carried My love for you to My death. Did I make the right decision, to pay the ultimate price for love? Of course I did. What else would I do, given the wonderful creation that is you? In the same way, I want each of My apostles to expect his love for Me to be a burden to him at times. This is normal. I want each of My apostles to expect his love for others to be a burden to him at times. This is also normal. In love, there are times when the decision to love feels light, of course, and there seems to be no burden to it at all. Rejoice in these times. In love, there are other times when the bur-

den causes you to question your commitment. Do not be afraid of these times. This questioning is necessary for your growth. I experienced this, too. I was tempted toward an easier way. When love is tried this way and triumphs, that love becomes firmer and less likely to be disappointed later. Welcome the challenges to love, even while you decide for love. I will be with you in each situation, counseling you to humility and gentleness. View each challenge as a worthy exercise, allowed by heaven to teach you about eternity. See the opportunities to love all of those around you, particularly those whom you find it difficult to agree with at times. Please do not be alarmed when you are disappointed in love, when others fail you. This was also My experience and this will also benefit you because it will help you to learn forgiveness. I will bring you to greater holiness with each experience if you remember that I am with you and that I love you perfectly and completely. From the secure place that is My heart, you will go forward with self-assurance, confident that you are cherished. This confidence will express itself in an increased ability to love those around you. Be at peace, dear apostles. My plan is such that you will learn to live like residents of heaven. All is well.

Jesus

My dear apostles, I speak to you from My heart, the seat of love. I speak to you freely at this time to teach you about love. I desire that each of you accept My love, which includes the love of all of heaven. Those who are lukewarm and do not accept my love cannot help Me in My goal of renewal. Those who are concerned with establishing their kingdoms on earth will lose opportunities to seed the renewal each day. Those who postpone a full commitment to My goals will find that they are sadly disappointed later, when they realize how important their service was to Me. I rely on My apostles to be passionate about service, seeking always to store up heavenly treasures in the souls of those around them. Truly, no kind word, no compassionate silence, no act of love is lost. Each of these is both used immediately and preserved eternally. I understand that you are tired at times. I understand that you become discouraged. I understand these things because in My humanity I experienced these things. I allow these feelings in My beloved apostles because their service to Me then becomes even more beneficial. Rest assured that you have been given all that you need in strength and courage for each day's service. There is no difficulty, from heaven's perspective, in an apostle serving in weariness. Most apostles served in weariness and the weariness that an apostle feels does not mean that the fire of the Spirit is at risk of being extinguished. Have no fear about this because I Myself tend to the presence of the Spirit in your soul. This fire has been expertly banked so that it will burn for as long as it needs to burn. Some day you will be finished with your service on earth. The tasks that I need from you will be completed. This will be a joyful day for you. You will see all that you have accomplished for Me. Yes, weariness comes and goes, but love creates stamina that keeps the servant and the service steady. In the time to come I intend to increase the capacity for love in each apostle. This is necessary for heaven's goals and will enable My beloved ones to serve with even greater dedication and humility. I will teach you more and instruct you closely in the use of this gift as time passes. This heavenly concession will greatly increase the effectiveness of My presence in your soul. I am so grateful that you seek to remain close to Me. Rejoice, dear apostles. I am with you.

Jesus

Dear apostles, My heart is bursting with love for each one of you. Indeed, I cannot contain the love that I possess for all of mankind. Many reject My love. They are not open to accepting love directly from My heart. You, My beloved apostles serving in this time, do accept the love of the Savior. You rejoice in My love. You allow My love to transform you into carriers of heaven's healing plan for humanity. Because so many reject Me, I give in a ridiculously lavish way to those willing to accept Me. Many of God's children, living in the sadness of sin, will not admit that God could offer them anything of value. They are closed to My love for them and they are closed to My plan for them. But these people will, nevertheless, accept kindness from you, God's apostles. They will accept good example from you, God's apostles. Ultimately, if My plan is successful, they will accept love from you. The love they find in your heart will belong to Me because I placed it there. When the people around you are loved by you, they experience Me. This works because you are connected to Me each day through your apostolic pledge and through your apostolic service. I have told you in the past that you bring light to a dark world. I want you to know, dear loyal apostles, that the light you bring is changing the world. We, those of us in heaven, see the light growing. Some of you begin un-

steadily. You are not certain that you are called. My beloved one, I am speaking to you now. Listen to Me. You are called. You belong in this family. I need your help. I do not ever want to be apart from you again. It hurts Me to be apart from you and it hurts you to be apart from Me. Only I love you perfectly. If you remain close to Me, I can continue to love you in such in a way that you will value yourself as heaven values you. You are not perfect. It is true. I accept this about you. If you believed you were perfect, My beloved friend, you would be no good to Me. Far better for every one of My goals that you believe you are flawed. Believe in My perfection and be willing, and together we will bring an unstoppable flow of love into the world. I rejoice in your love for Me, dear apostle. I want you to rejoice in My love for you. If you do this, you will show others an accurate example of the peace that comes from resting in the Savior. Rejoice in your heart. I am there and I love you.

Jesus

June 1, 2008

I am here, with you at all times. I watch you struggle for holiness and I encourage you to continue along on the path you have chosen. When you are discouraged, you sometimes look to other paths, chosen by other people. From where you are looking, their path might look smooth and easy, happy and fulfilling. Perhaps their path does not include the sacrifices that you find are necessary to travel along the path I have marked out for you. Perhaps their path does not appear to be as steep, as filled with obstacles, and perhaps their path appears to include more worldly acclaim and acceptance. Poor little apostles. Here is what you cannot see when you admire the apparent easiness of the paths of others who are not chosen as you are chosen. You do not see that others, who have not made the same level of commitment, are not enjoying the same level of unity with heaven. Yes, their struggle seems less. Yes, their rewards seem immediate and plentiful. But you have something that nobody else has in the same way and that is Me. Nobody has the same relationship with Me that you have. You are My beloved apostle and I love all of My apostles. But the love I have for you and the plan I have for you is unique. It will never be repeated. I need you to continue on in your service to Me. I need you to remember that you are called to live differently, that your life, which may not be proceeding exactly as you planned, is proceeding exactly as I planned. Can you accept this? Can you remind yourself that you have allowed your Savior to navigate your earthly journey? Can you rejoice in the path that I have marked out for you, even if it includes suffering? Please, My beloved apostle, try. I will help you with this. Rejoice in your apostolic commitment to Me. I will send you graces in each moment. These graces are unrepeatable, meaning that if a person rejects My grace in this moment, that grace moment cannot be recaptured. Time passes while you are on earth. Opportunities also pass. You are taking advantage of your time on earth for the family of God and for your loved ones and for you, yourself. You are so precious to Me. I am caring for you, I promise. When you are tempted to discouragement, remember that I am with you in each moment, sending perfect graces and blessings to you and through you. Be at peace in My will for you and I will protect My plan for you. You are loved by all of heaven and you are loved by Me.

Appendix

Guidelines for Lay Apostles

As lay apostles of Jesus Christ the Returning King, we agree to perform our basic obligations as practicing Catholics. Additionally, we will adopt the following spiritual practices, as best we can:

1. **Allegiance Prayer** and **Morning Offering**, plus a brief prayer for the Holy Father
2. **Eucharistic Adoration**, one hour per week
3. **Prayer Group Participation**, monthly, at which we pray the Luminous Mysteries of the Holy Rosary and read the Monthly Message
4. **Monthly Confession**
5. Further, we will follow the example of Jesus Christ as set out in the Holy Scripture, treating all others with His patience and kindness.

Allegiance Prayer

Dear God in heaven, I pledge my allegiance to You. I give You my life, my work and my heart. In turn, give me the grace of obeying Your every direction to the fullest possible extent. Amen.

Morning Offering

O Jesus, through the Immaculate Heart of Mary, I offer You the prayers, works, joys and sufferings of this day, for all the intentions of Your Sacred Heart, in union with the Holy Sacrifice of the Mass throughout the world, in reparation for my sins, and for the intentions of the Holy Father. Amen.

Prayer for the Holy Father

Blessed Mother of Jesus, protect our Holy Father, Benedict XVI, and bless his intentions.

Five Luminous Mysteries

1. The Baptism of Jesus
2. The Wedding at Cana
3. The Proclamation of the Kingdom of God
4. The Transfiguration
5. The Institution of the Eucharist

Promise from Jesus to His Lay Apostles

May 12, 2005

Your message to souls remains constant. Welcome each soul to the rescue mission. You may assure each lay apostle that just as they concern themselves with My interests, I will concern Myself with theirs. They will be placed in My Sacred Heart and I will defend and protect them. I will also pursue complete conversion of each of their loved ones. So you see, the souls who serve in this rescue mission as My beloved lay apostles will know peace. The world cannot make this promise as only heaven can bestow peace on a soul. This is truly heaven's mission and I call every one of heaven's children to assist Me. You will be well rewarded, My dear ones.

Prayers Taken from The Volumes

Prayers to God the Father

"I trust You, God. I offer You my pain in the spirit of acceptance and I will serve You in every circumstance."

"God my Father in heaven, You are all mercy. You love me and see my every sin. God, I call on You now as the Merciful Father. Forgive my every sin. Wash away the stains on my soul so that I may once again rest in complete innocence. I trust You, Father in heaven. I rely on You. I thank You. Amen."

"God my Father, calm my spirit and direct my path."

"God, I have made mistakes. I am sorry. I am Your child, though, and seek to be united to You."

"I believe in God. I believe Jesus is calling me. I believe my Blessed Mother has requested my help. Therefore I am going to pray on this day and every day."

"God my Father, help me to understand."

Prayers to Jesus

"Jesus, I give You my day."

"Jesus, how do You want to use me on this day? You have a willing servant in me, Jesus. Allow me to work for the kingdom."

"Lord, what can I do today to prepare for Your coming? Direct me, Lord, and I will see to Your wishes."

"Lord, help me."

"Jesus, love me."

Prayers to the Angels

"Angels from heaven, direct my path."

"Dearest angel guardian, I desire to serve Jesus by remaining at peace. Please obtain for me the graces necessary to maintain His divine peace in my heart."

Prayers for a Struggling Soul

"Jesus, what do You think of all this? Jesus, what do You want me to do for this soul? Jesus, show me how to bring You into this situation."

"Angel guardian, thank you for your constant vigil over this soul. Saints in heaven, please assist this dear angel."

Prayers for Children

"God in heaven, You are the Creator of all things. Please send Your graces down upon our world."

"Jesus, I love You."

"Jesus, I trust in You. Jesus, I trust in You. Jesus, I trust in You."

"Jesus, I offer You my day."

"Mother Mary, help me to be good."

How to Recite the Chaplet of Divine Mercy

The Chaplet of Mercy is recited using ordinary Rosary beads of five decades. The Chaplet is preceded by two opening prayers from the *Diary* of Saint Faustina and followed by a closing prayer.

1. Make the Sign of the Cross

In the name of the Father, and of the Son, and of the Holy Spirit. Amen.

2. Optional Opening Prayers

You expired, Jesus, but the source of life gushed forth for souls, and the ocean of mercy opened up for the whole world. O Fount of Life, unfathomable Divine Mercy, envelop the whole world and empty Yourself out upon us.

O Blood and Water, which gushed forth from the Heart of Jesus as a fountain of mercy for us, I trust in You!

3. Our Father

Our Father, who art in heaven, hallowed be Thy name. Thy kingdom come. Thy will be done on earth as it is in heaven. Give us this day our daily bread. And forgive us our trespasses, as we forgive those who trespass against us. And lead us not into temptation, but deliver us from evil. Amen.

4. Hail Mary

Hail Mary, full of grace, the Lord is with thee. Blessed art thou among women, and blessed is the fruit of thy womb, Jesus. Holy Mary, Mother of God, pray for us sinners, now and at the hour of our death. Amen.

5. The Apostles' Creed

I believe in God, the Father Almighty, Creator of heaven and earth. I believe in Jesus Christ, His only Son, Our Lord. He was conceived by the power of the Holy Spirit and born of the Virgin Mary. He suffered under Pontius Pilate, was crucified, died, and was buried. He descended to the dead. On the third day He rose again. He ascended into heaven, and is seated at the right hand of the Father. He will come again to judge the living and the dead. I believe in the Holy Spirit, the holy Catholic Church, the Communion of Saints, the forgiveness of sins, the resurrection of the body, and life everlasting. Amen.

6. The Eternal Father

Eternal Father, I offer You the Body and Blood, Soul and Divinity of Your Dearly Beloved Son, Our Lord, Jesus Christ, in atonement for our sins and those of the whole world.

7. On the Ten Small Beads of Each Decade

For the sake of His Sorrowful Passion, have mercy on us and on the whole world.

8. Repeat for the remaining decades

Saying the "Eternal Father" (6) on the "Our Father" bead and then 10 "For the sake of His Sorrowful Passion" (7) on the following "Hail Mary" beads.

9. Conclude with Holy God

Holy God, Holy Mighty One, Holy Immortal One, have mercy on us and on the whole world.

10. Optional Closing Prayer

Eternal God, in whom mercy is endless and the treasury of compassion—inexhaustible, look kindly upon us and increase Your mercy in us, that in difficult moments we might not despair nor become despondent, but with great confidence submit ourselves to Your holy will, which is Love and Mercy itself.

To learn more about the image of The Divine Mercy, the Chaplet of Divine Mercy and the series of revelations given to St. Faustina Kowalska please contact:

Marians of the Immaculate Conception
Stockbridge, Massachusetts 01263
Telephone 800-462-7426
www.marian.org

How to Pray the Rosary

1. Make the Sign of the Cross and say the "Apostles Creed."
2. Say the "Our Father."
3. Say three "Hail Marys."
4. Say the "Glory be to the Father."
5. Announce the First Mystery; then say the "Our Father."
6. Say ten "Hail Marys," while meditating on the Mystery.
7. Say the "Glory be to the Father." After each decade say the following prayer requested by the Blessed Virgin Mary at Fatima: "O my Jesus, forgive us our sins, save us from the fires of hell, lead all souls to Heaven, especially those in most need of Thy mercy."
8. Announce the Second Mystery: then say the "Our Father." Repeat 6 and 7 and continue with the Third, Fourth, and Fifth Mysteries in the same manner.
9. Say the "Hail, Holy Queen" on the medal after the five decades are completed.

As a general rule, depending on the season, the Joyful Mysteries are said on Monday and Saturday; the Sorrowful Mysteries on Tuesday and Friday; the Glorious Mysteries on Wednesday and Sunday; and the Luminous Mysteries on Thursday.

Papal Reflections of the Mysteries

The Joyful Mysteries

The Joyful Mysteries are marked by the joy radiating from the event of the Incarnation. This is clear from the very first mystery, the Annunciation, where Gabriel's greeting to the Virgin of Nazareth is linked to an invitation to messianic joy: "Rejoice, Mary." The whole of salvation... had led up to this greeting.

(Prayed on Mondays and Saturdays, and optional on Sundays during Advent and the Christmas Season.)

The Luminous Mysteries

Moving on from the infancy and the hidden life in Nazareth to the public life of Jesus, our contemplation brings us to those mysteries which may be called in a special way "mysteries of light." Certainly, the whole mystery of Christ is a mystery of light. He is the "Light of the world" (John 8:12). Yet this truth emerges in a special way during the years of His public life. (Prayed on Thursdays.)

The Sorrowful Mysteries

The Gospels give great prominence to the Sorrowful Mysteries of Christ. From the beginning, Christian piety, especially during the Lenten devotion of the Way of the Cross, has focused on the individual moments of the Passion, realizing that here is found the culmination of the revelation of God's love and the source of our salvation. (Prayed on Tuesdays and Fridays, and optional on Sundays during Lent.)

The Glorious Mysteries

"The contemplation of Christ's face cannot stop at the image of the Crucified One. He is the Risen One!" The Rosary has always expressed this knowledge born of faith and invited the believer to pass beyond the darkness of the Passion in order to gaze upon Christ's glory in the Resurrection and Ascension... Mary herself would be raised to that same glory in the Assumption. (Prayed on Wednesdays and Sundays.)

From the *Apostolic Letter The Rosary of the Virgin Mary*, Pope John Paul II, Oct. 16, 2002.

Prayers of the Rosary

The Sign of the Cross
In the name of the Father, and of the Son, and of the Holy Spirit. Amen.

The Apostles' Creed
I believe in God, the Father Almighty, Creator of heaven and earth. I believe in Jesus Christ, His only Son, Our Lord. He was conceived by the power of the Holy Spirit and born of the Virgin Mary. He suffered under Pontius Pilate, was crucified, died, and was buried. He descended to the dead. On the third day He rose again. He ascended into heaven, and is seated at the right hand of the Father. He will come again to judge the living and the dead. I believe in the Holy Spirit, the holy Catholic Church, the Communion of Saints, the forgiveness of sins, the resurrection of the body, and life everlasting. Amen.

Our Father
Our Father, who art in heaven, hallowed be Thy name. Thy kingdom come. Thy will be done on earth as it is in heaven. Give us this day our daily bread. And forgive us our trespasses, as we forgive those who trespass against us. And lead us not into temptation, but deliver us from evil. Amen.

Hail Mary
Hail Mary, full of grace, the Lord is with thee. Blessed art thou among women, and blessed is the fruit of thy womb, Jesus. Holy Mary, Mother of God, pray for us sinners, now and at the hour of our death. Amen.

Glory Be to the Father
Glory be to the Father, and to the Son, and to the Holy Spirit. As it was in the beginning, is now, and ever shall be, world without end. Amen.

Hail Holy Queen

Hail, Holy Queen, Mother of Mercy, our life, our sweetness and our hope. To thee do we cry, poor banished children of Eve. To thee do we send up our sighs, mourning and weeping in this valley of tears. Turn then, most gracious Advocate, thine eyes of mercy towards us. And after this, our exile, show unto us the blessed fruit of thy womb, Jesus. O clement, O loving, O sweet Virgin Mary!

Pray for us, O Holy Mother of God.
That we may be made worthy of the promises of Christ.

The Mysteries

First Joyful Mystery:
The Annunciation

And when the angel had come to her, he said, "Hail, full of grace, the Lord is with thee. Blessed art thou among women."

(Luke 1:28)

One *Our Father*, Ten *Hail Marys*,
One *Glory Be*, etc.

Fruit of the Mystery: ***Humility***

Second Joyful Mystery:
The Visitation

Elizabeth was filled with the Holy Spirit and cried out in a loud voice: "Blest are you among women and blest is the fruit of your womb." *(Luke* 1:41-42)

One *Our Father*, Ten *Hail Marys*,
One *Glory Be*, etc.

Fruit of the Mystery: ***Love of Neighbor***

Third Joyful Mystery:
The Birth of Jesus

She gave birth to her first-born Son and wrapped Him in swaddling clothes and laid Him in a manger, because there was no room for them in the place where travelers lodged.   (*Luke* 2:7)

One *Our Father*, Ten *Hail Marys*,
One *Glory Be*, etc.

Fruit of the Mystery: ***Poverty***

Fourth Joyful Mystery:
The Presentation

When the day came to purify them according to the law of Moses, the couple brought Him up to Jerusalem so that He could be presented to the Lord, for it is written in the law of the Lord, "Every first-born male shall be consecrated to the Lord."

(*Luke* 2:22-23)

One *Our Father*, Ten *Hail Marys*,
One *Glory Be*, etc.

Fruit of the Mystery: ***Obedience***

Fifth Joyful Mystery:
The Finding of the Child Jesus in the Temple

On the third day they came upon Him in the temple sitting in the midst of the teachers, listening to them and asking them questions.   (*Luke* 2:46)

One *Our Father*, Ten *Hail Marys*,
One *Glory Be*, etc.

Fruit of the Mystery: ***Joy in Finding Jesus***

First Luminous Mystery:
The Baptism of Jesus

And when Jesus was baptized... the heavens were opened and He saw the Spirit of God descending like a dove, and alighting on Him, and lo, a voice from heaven, saying "this is My beloved Son," with whom I am well pleased."   (*Matthew* 3:16-17)

One *Our Father*, Ten *Hail Marys*,
One *Glory Be*, etc.

Fruit of the Mystery: ***Openness to the Holy Spirit***

Second Luminous Mystery:
The Wedding at Cana

His mother said to the servants, "Do whatever He tells you." . . .
Jesus said to them, "Fill the jars with water." And they filled them
up to the brim.

(John 2:5-7)

One Our Father, Ten Hail Marys,
One Glory Be, etc.

Fruit of the Mystery: ***To Jesus through Mary***

Third Luminous Mystery:
The Proclamation of the Kingdom of God

"And preach as you go, saying, 'The kingdom of heaven is at
hand.' Heal the sick, raise the dead, cleanse lepers, cast out
demons. You received without pay, give without pay."

(Matthew 10:7-8)

One Our Father, Ten Hail Marys,
One Glory Be, etc.

Fruit of the Mystery: ***Repentance and Trust in God***

Fourth Luminous Mystery:
The Transfiguration

And as He was praying, the appearance of His countenance was
altered and His raiment become dazzling white. And a voice came
out of the cloud saying, "This is My Son, My chosen; listen to Him!

(Luke 9:29, 35)

One Our Father, Ten Hail Marys,
One Glory Be, etc.

Fruit of the Mystery: ***Desire for Holiness***

Fifth Luminous Mystery:
The Institution of the Eucharist

And He took bread, and when He had given thanks He broke it and gave it to them, saying, "This is My body which is given for you." . . . And likewise the cup after supper, saying, "This cup which is poured out for you is the new covenant in My blood."

(Luke 22:19-20)

One *Our Father*, Ten *Hail Marys*,
One *Glory Be*, etc.

Fruit of the Mystery: *Adoration*

First Sorrowful Mystery:
The Agony in the Garden

In His anguish He prayed with all the greater intensity, and His sweat became like drops of blood falling to the ground. Then He rose from prayer and came to His disciples, only to find them asleep, exhausted with grief.   (*Luke* 22:44-45)

One *Our Father*, Ten *Hail Marys*,
One *Glory Be*, etc.

Fruit of the Mystery: *Sorrow for Sin*

Second Sorrowful Mystery:
The Scourging at the Pillar

Pilate's next move was to take Jesus and have Him scourged.

(*John* 19:1)

One *Our Father*, Ten *Hail Marys*,
One *Glory Be*, etc.

Fruit of the Mystery: *Purity*

Third Sorrowful Mystery:
The Crowning with Thorns

They stripped off His clothes and wrapped Him in a scarlet military cloak. Weaving a crown out of thorns they fixed it on His head, and stuck a reed in His right hand...   (Matthew 27:28-29)

One *Our Father*, Ten *Hail Marys*,
One *Glory Be*, etc.

Fruit of the Mystery: *Courage*

**Fourth Sorrowful Mystery:
The Carrying of the Cross**

... carrying the cross by Himself, He went out to what is called the Place of the Skull (in Hebrew, Golgotha).   (*John* 19:17)
One *Our Father*, Ten *Hail Marys*,
One *Glory Be*, etc.
Fruit of the Mystery: *Patience*

**Fifth Sorrowful Mystery:
The Crucifixion**

Jesus uttered a loud cry and said, "Father, into Your hands I commend My spirit." After He said this, He expired.   (*Luke* 23:46)
One *Our Father*, Ten *Hail Marys*,
One *Glory Be*, etc.
Fruit of the Mystery: *Perseverance*

**First Glorious Mystery:
The Resurrection**

You need not be amazed! You are looking for Jesus of Nazareth, the one who was crucified. He has been raised up; He is not here. See the place where they laid Him."   (*Mark* 16:6)
One *Our Father*, Ten *Hail Marys*,
One *Glory Be*, etc.
Fruit of the Mystery: *Faith*

**Second Glorious Mystery:
The Ascension**

Then, after speaking to them, the Lord Jesus was taken up into Heaven and took His seat at God's right hand.   (*Mark* 16:19)
One *Our Father*, Ten *Hail Marys*,
One *Glory Be*, etc.
Fruit of the Mystery: *Hope*

Third Glorious Mystery:
The Descent of the Holy Spirit

All were filled with the Holy Spirit. They began to express themselves in foreign tongues and make bold proclamation as the Spirit prompted them. (*Acts* 2:4)

One *Our Father*, Ten *Hail Marys*,
One *Glory Be*, etc.

Fruit of the Mystery: **Love of God**

Fourth Glorious Mystery:
The Assumption

You are the glory of Jerusalem... you are the splendid boast of our people... God is pleased with what you have wrought. May you be blessed by the Lord Almighty forever and ever.

(*Judith* 15:9-10)

One *Our Father*, Ten *Hail Marys*,
One *Glory Be*, etc.

Fruit of the Mystery: **Grace of a Happy Death**

Fifth Glorious Mystery:
The Coronation

A great sign appeared in the sky, a woman clothed with the sun, with the moon under her feet, and on her head a crown of twelve stars. (*Revelation* 12:1)

One *Our Father*, Ten *Hail Marys*,
One *Glory Be*, etc.

Fruit of the Mystery: **Trust in Mary's Intercession**

The Volumes
Direction for Our Times
as given to Anne, a lay apostle

Volume One: *Thoughts on Spirituality*
Volume Two: *Conversations with the*
Eucharistic Heart of Jesus
Volume Three: *God the Father Speaks to*
His Children
The Blessed Mother Speaks
to Her Bishops and Priests
Volume Four: *Jesus the King*
Heaven Speaks to Priests
Jesus Speaks to Sinners
Volume Six: *Heaven Speaks to Families*
Volume Seven: *Greetings from Heaven*
Volume Nine: *Angels*
Volume Ten: *Jesus Speaks to His Apostles*

Volumes 5 and 8 will be printed at a later date.

The Volumes are now available in PDF format
for free download and printing from our website:
www.directionforourtimes.org.
We encourage everyone to print and distribute them.

The Volumes are also available at your local bookstore.

The *Heaven Speaks* Booklets
Direction for Our Times
as given to Anne, a lay apostle

The following booklets are available individually from Direction for Our Times:

Heaven Speaks About Abortion
Heaven Speaks About Addictions
Heaven Speaks to Victims of Clerical Abuse
Heaven Speaks to Consecrated Souls
Heaven Speaks About Depression
Heaven Speaks About Divorce
Heaven Speaks to Prisoners
Heaven Speaks to Soldiers
Heaven Speaks About Stress
Heaven Speaks to Young Adults

Heaven Speaks to Those Away from the Church
Heaven Speaks to Those Considering Suicide
Heaven Speaks to Those Who Do Not Know Jesus
Heaven Speaks to Those Who Are Dying
Heaven Speaks to Those Who Experience Tragedy
Heaven Speaks to Those Who Fear Purgatory
Heaven Speaks to Those Who Have Rejected God
Heaven Speaks to Those Who Struggle to Forgive
Heaven Speaks to Those Who Suffer from Financial Need
Heaven Speaks to Parents Who Worry About
**   Their Children's Salvation**

All twenty of the *Heaven Speaks* booklets are now available for free download and printing from our website www.directionforourtimes.org. We encourage everyone to print and distribute these booklets.

Other Written Works by Anne, a lay apostle

Climbing the Mountain

This book contains the fascinating story of how the rescue mission began and how it has blossomed into a worldwide apostolate under the watchful eye and in complete obedience to the Church. It is the story of The Lay Apostolate of Jesus Christ the Returning King.

Also featured is a summary of Anne's mystical experiences of heaven. She describes the heavenly home that has been created for God's children. Reading these accounts, you will learn that in heaven we will experience constant unity with Jesus. Anne also confirms that souls in heaven work together to assist in answering the prayers of God's earthly children. At one point in time Jesus tells Anne, *"...you are a child of God and you have every right to be here."*

In the section entitled "Climbing the Mountain," Anne writes about her vision of the personal call to holiness that we all must hear.

It concludes with a reprint of the first ten "Heaven Speaks" booklets: Abortion, Addictions, Victims of Clerical Abuse, Consecrated Souls, Depression, Divorce, Prisoners, Soldiers, Stress, and Young Adults.

This is a book to be treasured as it reveals the intimate love of the Savior for each soul. Every reader will be called to great rejoicing, for truly, God's kingdom comes.

The Mist of Mercy

Anne begins this full-length book by telling us that the enemy of God is present on earth and a battle is being waged for souls. Satan is trying to destroy God's plan for us, which is unity with Him in heaven for eternity. We must be alert to these efforts and be armed for the battle. This is the reality of spiritual warfare.

Following is a section entitled *Snapshots of Reality* which is a collection of short stories depicting realistic earthly struggles while including a glimpse of these same situations from the heavenly perspective and how our friends, the saints, act on our behalf more than we can imagine.

Also in this book is Anne's account of her mystical experiences of purgatory. She tells us of the souls she saw there and describes the prayers they prayed and the remorse they felt for the choices they had made on earth which were against the will of God. You will be happy to learn that purgatory is a great mercy of God and allows each soul there the perfect experience of preparation for eternity in heaven.

The last section is a reprint of the Monthly Messages from Jesus Christ dated from December 1, 2004 through June 1, 2006.

Interviews with Anne, a lay apostle

VHS tapes and DVDs featuring Anne, a lay apostle, have been produced by Focus Worldwide Network and can be purchased by visiting our website at:

www.directionforourtimes.org

This book is part of a non-profit mission.
Our Lord has requested that we
spread these words internationally.

Please help us.

If you would like to assist us financially,
please send your tax-deductible contribution
to the address below:

Direction for Our Times
9000 West 81st Street
Justice, Illinois 60458

www.directionforourtimes.org

Email: contactus@directionforourtimes.com
Phone: 708-496-9300

Direction for Our Times—Ireland
Drumacarrow
Bailieborough
Co. Cavan.
Republic of Ireland

www.directionforourtimes.org

Email: dfotireland@eircom.net
Phone: 353-(0)42-969-4947

Direction for Our Times is a 501(c)(3)
not-for-profit corporation. Contributions are
deductible to the extent provided by law.

Jesus gives Anne a message for the world on
the first of each month. To receive the
monthly messages you may access our
website at www.directionforourtimes.org
or call us at 708-496-9300
to be placed on our mailing list.